Explaining the Unexplainable:
How One Anti-theist Skeptic Looks at Mysteries

By J.M. Ladd
©2010

Other Books by J.M. Ladd

The Bitter Pill of Truth: A Cure for Judeo-Christianity

Please visit www.bitterpilloftruth.com

Contents

Preface

The universe is a pretty amazing place. Events have happened, are happening and will continue to happen that confound, bewilder, baffle and amaze us. There are tangible things in this universe, objects and creatures, which fall into the same categories. Despite that the human race has been around for the comparative eye-blink in the universe's history, we have discovered quite a bit about many, many things. Still, there are questions that haunt us, keep us up late at night and cause us to pause and consider. I believe that, in time, just about all things will be explained by science. I say "just about" because I also believe that some things may always be beyond our comprehension. Nothing is perfect and some things will never be complete; in this case I argue it is knowledge that will never be complete. Whether it is human knowledge, the knowledge of an alien species, or even the combined, I do not believe sentient creatures will ever know all there is to know. That, of course, is what drives scientists; discovery and invention. I say this not from a supernatural, religious standpoint, but from that of an anti-theist.

The purpose of this book is not to change a person's mind regarding their religious views. This book *is not* meant to deal with religions in regards to their moral teachings, veracity, dogma, or substance. This book *is* meant for people to look at what we deem the unexplained and the supernatural through different eye sand from a different viewpoint—mine. The premise of this book is how **I**, an anti-theist, look at the unexplained in regards to **my** own non-religious ways. If you are strong and devout in your faith, great! If you are lacking in it, or have none (as with me), great! If you happen to change your religious views because of this book, well… I cannot say that I would be disappointed (the world needs more non-believers) but this book was not meant to be a conversion tool.

Each and every chapter of this book deals with a substance that merits a whole book of its own and indeed there are volumes and volumes out there, but I am writing this book to be a quick and hopefully fun read. It is more of a handbook than a deep, delving look into the mysterious and the unexplained.

To continue with this book, please allow me to explain anti-theism, atheism and agnosticism versus religiosity in an easy way and one that will not put you to sleep. You must understand what it is to be an anti-theist to follow the logic of all my coming arguments and opinions on mysteries and the unexplained.

As we all know, religion means that a set of values, tenant sand beliefs shape a person's moral and world views. Almost every religion that has ever been practiced on this world has included a god (or gods) that governs and dictates how the religion should be followed. Atheism relates to the Judeo-Christian and Islamic god—God, Yahweh, Allah, Adonai, the Lord, etc… Atheism simply means that a person does not acknowledge this god or the religion it represents. You will notice that the word god is only capitalized when speaking of this particular god. The word itself is not a formal noun, only when it is used to denote God, the god of the Jews, Christians and Islamic people.

Atheism is not a religion. No matter how many times it is compared to one, called one, or treated as one it is not a religion. Atheism has no tenants, no belief system or structure and no gods. It has no holy texts, no history to speak of and no claim other than that God does not exist. Atheists rely on reason, evidence and scientific knowledge, not upon faith. Atheists also refer to themselves as humanists and do what is decent and kind for the sake of goodness itself; reward or punishment does not factor into the equation, only that atheists are making the world a better, kinder place before we die.

An agnostic is what I like to call a religious fence-sitter. I can say that—with no malice intended—for a long time I considered myself to be an agnostic. An agnostic is someone who does not truly know in his or her own mind if any gods, more significantly God, exists. They would (possibly) like to believe in God and Heaven, but there is an equal amount of doubt coupled with a lack of evidence, so they sit on the fence. "Maybe there is a God and maybe there isn't; show me proof and evidence and I will gladly believe" is an agnostic's motto. Personally, I moved away from this belief because sitting on the fence is wishy-washy, or so I deemed. Make up your mind, take a stand, choose a side and play ball. Use reason, science and intelligence to determine what you believe and then live by that belief system.

Anti-theism is the disavowing of all gods, all religions and all dogmatic belief systems. It is atheism taken one step further. Like atheists, anti-theists are humanists and do not expend the mental energy worrying about Heaven, Hell, reward, punishment, final judgment and mortal sins. What concerns the anti-theist is kindness, tolerance, learning and science. It is the belief that we are all one race and that being moral and kind comes from living together and treating each other with respect for the sole reason that we all share this world and have a responsibility to it and to all upon it. That does not mean anti-theists are all pacifists, hippie sand tree-hungers.

We anti-theists like and dislike people and situations based on how we are treated and we, too, can be indifferent and cold to mean, hate-filled and spiteful people. We hunt, we fish, we eat meat, we wear leather and fur and we are policemen, firemen, judges, doctors and soldiers. We are also vegetarians, teachers, lawyers, scientists, peace-craving, anti-hunting, anti-leather and fur, PETA-belonging members of society. Some of us are Democrats, some Republicans and some Independents. We are liberals, conservatives and moderates. We can be politically correct just as we can despise political correctness. In short, we are everyone, from all corners of this world and come from and lead all walks of life. Anti-theists do not waste time with religions as we find them pointless, meaningless, meritless and pretty much all morally bankrupt.

With all that out of the way we are free to continue to the great mysteries we humans are faced with on this third rock from the sun. To be more accurate I like to call mysteries the unexplained and the "supernatural" misunderstandings. This short handbook is more opinion than actual, empirical, hard-evidenced fact, but looking at mysteries with your anti-theist glasses on mysteries become less mysterious and more mentally manageable. Some may even make perfect sense!

Chapter One: Gods

The first chapter's substance should be glaringly obvious and so we must start at the top: gods. This book's observations are based on the atheistic/anti-theistic view that there are no gods, especially God. I say especially God because God is the most popular deity of all time.

Why do non-believers not believe in gods? Simply put, there is no hard evidence and no concrete proof. Faith itself is proof of nothing, no matter how many people have it. Think of it this way: I have a dog. Her name is Haika, and she is a three-year old Yorkshire terrier. I fully believe in my heart of hearts that when I leave to go do errands that Haika flies about the house. She literally flies, soaring all about and playing when no one is home. I whole-heartedly, unequivocally and faithfully believe that. I cannot prove it with empirical evidence and have never caught her, but I know it to be true. Every fiber of my being tells me she does this. Does that sound crazy? If so, how dare anyone question my faith in this? It is what I choose to believe. Just because ancient, ignorant men did not write about this on stone tablets or upon paper long ago makes it untrue? What if I convinced four-billion people that Haika flies about the house when no one is home? Would that make my claim any more valid? The same holds true for all the gods with all their fantastic tales and histories that have ever been fabricated, including God. The burden to prove the supernatural and ultimately all fantastic claims lies upon the believer, not the non-believer. In my eyes, if you have to prove something and have but faith as your only evidence, you are facing an up-hill, losing battle.

Only when you realize that man has created all the gods that have ever been brought to life via mythology can you understand the coming chapters. At a young age, I developed two passions: paleontology and mythology. Just as I can rattle off the names, types, classifications, descriptions and characteristics of dozens and dozens of different dinosaurs, I can do the same for the gods of Earth's religions. As such, imagine if you will that all the gods are real.

Take Zeus, King of the Greek gods, as an example. The Greeks believed that enormous creatures called Titans created reality, including the first gods. Zeus was the oldest and strongest of the first gods. At some point, Zeus rallied the rest of his brother and sister deities and killed or enslaved all of the Titans. Once that was done, the gods procreated with one another and then made the world and then humans. In a nutshell, that is the story the Greeks grew up with. Roughly two-thousand years ago a new mythology came into being when Christianity was born.

Gods, whether fictional or real, are immortal and cannot die. They can, however, be forgotten. Imagine Zeus's anger at being replaced by the god of Abraham. Ignore Zeus, King of the Gods? Preposterous! Forget the great pantheon, including Hera, Hades and Poseidon? You would think that Zeus would once again rally his fellow Olympians and do to this new deity what he did to the Titans. What then of Odin, King of the Norse Gods and all his Asgardian kin? How about Ra, King of the Egyptian Gods and his great pantheon? I am sure the numerous and very war-like Aztec, Incan and Myan gods would have taken issue with God. There is a large Hindi pantheon of gods, many of them war-like and vigilant of their subjects, which is still followed to this day? What of all the pantheons of the world's religions that flourished at the time in human history when God came upon the scene? Would they not have declared war against God, even aligning with one another, to defeat and lay low this new, single deity? You could argue that God was/is just too powerful, or that the other gods are not real and God is the one true god, but that defense has holes.

For starters, God admits that other gods exist. All throughout the Bible God mentions how any and all other gods are to be ignored, and that homage should be paid only to God Himself; He is a self-proclaimed jealous deity. Moreover God is so jealous that He makes numerous commands (in the Bible) that all followers of other gods should be put to death. Even the first of the Ten Commandments says, "Thou shall have no other gods but Me." God should have commanded "There *are* no other gods but Me." All this is evidence that God acknowledges that other gods exist. If this is so and God is the one true god, then who made all the other gods? It must have been God. Why would He do such a thing and then make it an offense punishable by death to recognize the other gods? If He is as jealous as He touts Himself to be, why create any other gods in the first place? Even if these other deities existed before God (as unlikely as it seems if God is the one true god) why would God let them exist at all? The posers should have been erased from both history and memory...but they were not.

Next, there are no tales anywhere in the Bible, the Torah, the Gospels, in any known texts, or even in stories handed down throughout the generations about wars between God and any other god(s). If the other gods did make war against God—and lost—there is no mention of it anywhere...and if they did lose, they were never killed, destroyed, or erased from memory. To be perfectly technical, not a single religion is truly dead; they may have little or no followers at the moment, but that is subject to an over-night change.

The great mystery of a Prime Mover, or of pantheon of gods, is a veil. Gods are not real, but man-made creations to satisfy mortal, human longings for knowledge. Mankind needed answers to questions he could not answer. Why does it rain? What makes the earth quake so? Where did everything come from? Why are we experiencing a drought? What happens when we die? Perhaps gods were meant to be used as a coddling agent. Maybe religion is a built-in mechanism that aided in human survival and propagation of the species; mankind needs authoritative figures to get by, allow us to behave badly when we know better and to punish us when we are bad. Just as a parent tells a child not to put its finger in the socket, it is possible that early man needed superior gods to tell us how to act and behave.

Life and death were certainly different to humans two thousand years ago and earlier, as were morals, but mankind would have come to the conclusion that murder, rape, slavery and so forth are not good ways to live in a kind, functional society. We may have created our gods out of ignorance of science coupled with a developing sense of true moral behavior, but humankind outgrew gods a long time ago.

Now that I have argued, rather quickly, that gods do not and have never existed outside of human imagination, we can progress. Onward, then and put your thinking caps on!

Chapter Two: Ghosts

Since there are no gods, Heaven and Hell become moot points. The same goes for Valhalla, Hades, the Elysian Fields, Hell, the Summerland, the Underworld, and all other variations of where people think they go when they die. What then of ghosts, spirits and lost souls? If there is no afterlife, how can ghosts possibly exist? If there is no bright light, no "other side" and no crossing over how do we explain things that go bump in the night?

Before I get to that, please be aware of the fact that I personally do not believe that living creatures have souls. I cannot speak for all atheists and anti-theists, but a soul is something that is just too far-fetched in which for me to believe. I do not want to go into depth upon this as not to waste time—yours or mine—but suffice to say that my standpoint is that we are just creatures, children of the universe. We humans are animate matter, with a highly-evolved intelligence and a penchant for foolish, self-destructive behavior despite our brainpower. To possess a soul is just wishful thinking; an idea that was created by early humans out of fear of dying and what, if anything, happens after death. It is also ego, for if we have souls we can live forever in some form or another.

There is no hard, scientific proof that humans have souls. Believing we have them is akin to believing humans have invisible wings and can fly. One can site all the studies they wish, can recant all the stories of lore and can quote all the religious texts they choose, but direct and tangible evidence for a human soul does not exist. The same fact that faith is proof of nothing applies to souls.

If humans have no souls, how do we explain ghosts? Looking at ghosts, spooks, poltergeists and specters through my anti-theist goggles I see it all this way: You must take the scientific principles and laws that we have assigned to the universe into the equation. The most important of these rules comes from Albert Einstein and is his law of Conservation of Mass and Energy. For the layman, this law states that energy cannot be created or destroyed; it is always in existence and only changes form. The weight of the universe is constant and has never changed. The universe is as heavy now as it was at its inception.

Let us say I have a wall that is fifty-feet in height, five-feet thick and weighs fifty tons. The wall is made up entirely of wood. During a thunderstorm, a lightning strike ignites my wall and it bursts into flames. The wall burns to the ground and not a single timber is left. Is the wall gone? Of course not—what was once fifty tons of lumber has become a combined fifty tons of ash, dust and gasses. The wood did not disappear from the universe; it only changed its form. The ash and dust will blow about and settle somewhere to mix with the soil, or perhaps fall into a body of water where it will filter down to the seafloor or lake bottom. It will then mix with the sand or soil and become part of the plants that grow there. The gasses will mix with the air and water and form new molecules. Animals will ingest these plants and breathe in these molecules and add them to their mass.

The same holds true for a human body. When a person dies we decompose to become dust and gas. These molecules will find their way back into the cosmic pea soup that is the universe to help build other forms of matter. In that sense humans and all living things are truly immortal. The universe wastes nothing and everything is recycled.

So, if we have no soul, what happens to a person when we die? What of all the sightings and tales of ghosts? What of all the supposed evidence? To me, vintage black-and-white photographs of hazy, distorted human-like or amorphous shapes are not proof. EVP (electronic voice phenomenon) is sketchy at best. Eye-witness accounts are all hearsay. Television shows shot in old houses, castles, abandoned prisons, lighthouses and other places with actors using low-light cameras, military-style heat detectors and a semi-formal script are not only degrading to human intelligence, but are fake and not evidence of anything. I will probably repeat this line a dozen or more times throughout this book, but if we had solid, unadulterated evidence the issue would not be up for debate. I would not be writing this book and the skeptics would be silenced.

Why is it always some second or third party that always sees ghosts? Why is it always a fleeting glance, a cold spot in a room, or a hazy image? Why do not ghosts appear in well-lit, populated places? Why are they never on the five o'clock news and why do they never seek out reporters to tell their tales? If they want someone out of their home why do they never approach law enforcement, or an attorney?

Why are ghosts usually portrayed as evil, malignant and spiteful? Why do they always want people out of houses and why do they feel the need to spook and scare us by shaking tables, moving small objects about and making scary noises? It seems as if people die and if they become a ghost, they lose one-hundred or more I.Q. points.

Okay, so why do I not believe in ghosts? I am glad you asked. Since gods and an afterlife do not exist, nor does a human soul, ghosts are not really possible. There is no tangible proof of ghosts, no verifiable and credible evidence for them that science can study and there is no quantifiable way to prove souls are real outside of faith.

Every bit of the universe is made up of matter, and all matter is energy. I will concede that, since humans are made up of energy, we must obey the law that matter and energy are constant. When we die, the energy has to go somewhere. Psychic energy—another unproven theory, but that is for a later chapter—may or may not be real. If it is, it too, must succumb to Einstein's law. It has to be redistributed throughout the universe. Energy in its pure form has no physical body, no brain and no consciousness. Ghosts, as we believe them to be, are pure energy and are non-corporeal; that means they have no physical body and no brain. How then can ghosts have a consciousness, emotions and an agenda? It is not possible for a non-corporeal entity to have brain activity.

To produce sounds one needs the right equipment. In the case of a human voice, like moaning, shrieking, or spoken words a set of lungs, a diaphragm and a mouth are all needed. Ghosts, if real, have spectral body parts and do not have the right equipment to utter even the faintest whisper. In order to reproduce a single word, or the sound of a rattling chain, or whatever noise a spirit wants to spook the living with requires pure magic. Sounds cannot come from non-physical objects, and in order for a ghost to make a sound, speak a single word, or shriek the sound must be generated with a magical effect…and what of the sounds that ghostly machines and other objects make? Many people claim to hear rattling chains, footsteps, or the sound of phantom cars and vehicles. Such objects were never alive and could not possibly have spirits or a soul. How then do they create noises? How can a dead body recreate the visage and/or sounds of a length of steel chain or a complicated machine? Footsteps require physical weight and a body, but ghosts are spectral, non-corporeal beings and cannot possibly make the sound of a foot treading on the floor. The easiest and wisest explanation is that fearful and wantonly-superstitious people will make anything real to suit their fears and beliefs.

Can a ghost simply be the imprinting of energy upon this world? Yes, I suppose so, but that imprint would be like a stain. If you spill a glass of wine upon a white carpet, the wine is gone when it dries up and its molecules are recycled, but some of the molecules remain and form the stain. A ghost could be just an imprint of [psychic] energy left upon our corporeal world; a stain with no body, mind, emotions, or agenda. That is, of course, providing psychic energy is real and can be imprinted permanently on the universe. If it is and it can "stain" reality somehow, I suggest the stain would be an area with unstable or peculiar energy. This could explain a cold spot, but even that is a stretch.

A hot spot I could fathom and even believe. Energy means motion. All energy causes some sort of friction, from incalculable amounts to miniscule ones. One of the properties of energy is that light-emitting energy produces heat. Since light-emitting energy procures heat, any source that produces light must produce some amount of heat, no matter how insignificant. Light-energy cannot emit anti-heat. If a ghost is an imprint of energy left upon this universe why would it ever be cold? Even if the imprint is a hazy image of what was once a living person, whether a fully-formed torso or a ball of light, it would radiate heat energy because a visible image is a light-emitting form of energy. Light is radiation, radiation emits energy and energy that is emitted as radiation is warm.

Let me tell you why, in my humble opinion, cold spots and drops in temperature are always associated with ghosts: the cold of the grave.

Dead bodies do not radiate heat - rather they are cold and stiff. The chill of the grave is a favorite colloquialism among horror writers and the expression has long been used to express the disheartening fact that death's icy grip awaits us all. It is why vampires are always described as pale-skinned and cold to the touch. Although the subject of vampires will be tackled in a later chapter, Dracula gives us a credible detail in this case.

If I threw a dinner party and invited Count Dracula and he showed up with a ghost for a date—we will say the ghost of Mina Harker—energy-wise, he and his companion would be very different. As a vampire, Dracula is still made up of energy but his body is no longer alive; what was once a warm-blooded mammal is now a walking corpse without an active metabolism. Accordingly, his body would not generate heat and would be room temperature at best. My alive and functioning body, with its warm-blooded and active metabolism, would find Dracula's hand cold and clammy. Just as a piece of steel at room temperate seems cold to our 98.6° bodies, Dracula's hand would also be cool to the touch.

Mina on the other hand—no pun intended—would be an image, a projection of her former self. She would reach out as if to shake my hand, or have me gently kiss the front side of it, but alas, our hands would pass through one another. The sensation should not be one of cold; her image is made up of light-emitting energy and should be warm (room temperature at least). In order for me to even see Mina's visage there must be some physical substance she possesses with which to absorb energy and to re-emit it as her image. This suggests physical form. This creates a paradox that is solved when one realizes light-emitting non-corporeal entities that emit cold do not exist.

There exists another possibility to explain ghosts, but is fanciful at best. I cannot claim it as my own and it comes from the mind of novelist Anne Rice. In her wonderful book, *Memnoch the Devil*, Anne posits that God may have created the universe, including man, but ghosts and spirits were not in the plan. Anne's undead evolved independently of the plan for humankind via spiritual and psychic energy caused by death, loss, mourning and fear. Out of this combined lot of energy, ghosts formed.

From ghosts evolved the other forms of undead, ones that could take physical, corporeal form; vampires, ghouls, zombies, etc...

While I find the notion excitable and entertaining, it is still bizarre. I am all for the process of evolution, even in this extreme, but I just do not see it while wearing my anti-theistic goggles. Even if I took them off and abdicated a belief in gods, how could I not see ghosts and such as part of the plan?

Supposing ghosts are real, why would they desire only to haunt the living? Is there nothing better for them to do, or is this all their mental faculties can handle? Ghosts, like all things in the universe, are made up of energy. Energy in pure form is not bound by things such as gravity, or other movement restrictions, as living or solid matter are. Why stay here on this planet and bug the living? Why use cheap parlor tricks to scare humans and the occasional animal? Why not leave and travel the world, or explore whatever else is out there in the universe? Why keep living in the shadow of a former life and possibly revisiting the horror of a painful, tragic death every day for all eternity? Why do they need to be around the living if all they do is want us out of their territory, scare us, or disappear when we supposedly see them? The easiest explanation is that ghosts are but figments of human imagination and fear is the easiest emotion to play upon aside from greed.

It is our great, ingrained fear of death married to our unlimited penchant for creativity that has created the ghost. Humans see what they want to see, hear what they want to hear and believe what they want to believe in all manner of circumstances, most notably the supernatural. It is comforting to imagine that there is life after death and that some sort of better [after] life possibly awaits us. It is also intriguing and eerily thrilling, to suppose that a lost, tormented, or haunted spirit can stick around to either scare us or make us wonder.

For me my disbelief in gods does not allow me to believe in ghosts. Show me actual proof and I will happily change my tune; do not present to me some grainy photograph, or a supposed EVP, or tell me you saw one (because that is only hearsay no matter how credible or wonderful you are), or have me watch a lame television show - but show me a ghost.

Have a non-corporeal entity approach me, or bring me to a place where I can meet one face-to-face, somehow communicate with it while live television cameras roll that actually record the encounter and I will become a believer in ghosts. It will not change my theistic views, but it is a start.

Lastly, I cannot speak for other people who share my anti-theistic views, but all of the paragraphs above make it impossible for me to believe in reincarnation. Since humans do not possess a soul, there is no afterlife and gods are not real, reincarnation is just more wishful thinking. It is pleasing to think we humans can attain functional immortality by having an immortal soul returning to life until it is "truly happy" or "gets it right." I just do not prescribe to such nonsense.

All life is a natural part of this universe. Everything runs in cycles and the only immortality that living things attain is by having their energy and atoms never be truly destroyed but recycled by the universe; of course humans can attain limited immortality with their deeds, actions and works. Beethoven, Mozart, Galileo and Jules Verne will always be remembered. Genghis Khan, Julius Cesar, Bonnie and Clyde and Adolf Hitler will forever be remembered. Michelangelo, Michael Jackson, Michael Chriton, Michael Tyson and Sir Michael Caine have all been immortalized—for as long as humans exist, the famous and the infamous will have attained a form of immortality.

Speaking of infamy, to close this chapter I would like to touch on the subject of near-death experiences. It should go without saying that a person with no religion does not buy into near-death stories, but the one truth about the universe is that anything is possible, just highly unlikely. Death is frightening, even to those who do not fear final judgment or the various hells the religious believe in. It is the end of our lives and no one really wants to die. I am not afraid of dying, but I sure as hell do not want to. If I could live forever I would. I do not even care how it is, so long as my mind and my spirit—what I deem to be my moral code and every-day self—stay intact. If it were as a ghost and I was forced to "walk this earth forever" as a spectral being with no contact to other humans, I would have no problem with that. I would explore every corner and facet of this world, from people, places and cultures to wildlife and the mysterious deep blue oceans. I would become a voyeur of the living without being a terror or nuisance. Would I grow bored at some point? I am sure. Perhaps then I would spend my time trying to leave the bounds of this world and see if there is a way to travel to others, or even other realms, should they exist.

If I were to become a vampire and be forced to drink the blood of the living to be immortal, I would relish it. I would, of course, only prey upon the wicked, the base, and the criminal elements making this world a hell of a lot safer, but I would gladly do it. (Vampires come later in this book, so hold your judgment just now). I would love to endure forever, but that is not how life on earth operates.

A proven medical fact is that of the five senses that humans possess sight is the last to stop functioning when a person dies. The optic nerve sends signals to the brain during and even after death occurs, for a brief time. In that time a lot happens in terms of brain function, even when death is immediate. As the rods and cones of the eyes senses input and then translate the information to the brain along the optic nerve, the signals continue to travel and the fantastic mechanisms of the eye continue to work during and even after death. This span of time is but a few heartbeats, but enough for the brain to try and make sense of before it stops functioning.

As the eyes send signals to the dying brain, an experience akin to tunnel vision takes place. We lose definition in what we see, even loss of color vision. The signals are sparser and so we see "less", as if we had entered into a tunnel that was bright but is growing ever darker. It would and does seem as if the light is at the "end" of that tunnel and finally that light flares and winks out. This happens when we lose consciousness due to death, or to processes like medical anesthesia. It is not the light of Heaven we see when we black out or have a near death experience, but the nerves, neurons and signals firing from the eye to the brain and how the brain interprets these fading signals. The bright light we like to think of as heaven is just a mental sugar pill; no one really wants to die and so this is a coping mechanism we have created. We see what we want to see, what makes us comfortable and reassures us by whatever means necessary, that it is alright to die—hence we see loved ones, the face(s) of our chosen gods, the image of the gates of heaven, etc…

None of it is real. It makes us feel better about dying but it is not real. The experience people think they have, when they claim to have had a near-death experience, is only our sense of sight as it shuts down; plus the mantra of bright lights, heaven's gates and loved ones that we humans have instilled into our minds and into each generation.

Chapter Three: Magic

If you do not believe in gods then what becomes of magic? Without a source for magic to draw upon, does magic come from the universe itself? That seems highly unlikely, for if there are no gods and the universe is a natural phenomena, magic must also be a natural phenomena. That means that we enter into this barely credible situation: magic is a natural part of the universe and draws its power from the spoken word and from physical rituals and the gestures of sentient beings. This would have to mean that magic existed before life did and had waited billions of years for any world to form and support speech-capable life. It would also make magic a quasi-sentient energy source. That, of course, is absurd.

Another scientific law of the universe states that for every action there is an opposite and equal reaction. The energy that fuels magic has to come from somewhere. Since words and (usually) hand gestures are what fuel magical spells, are we to argue that the sonic vibrations created by human speech, along with the air displacement of hand and body gestures, make up magic's energy source? Or is it just the actual words that trigger magical effects. If so, why are these words only in ancient, dead, or even fake languages? Despite that it is pure fiction Harry Potter cannot just say "Fireball!" to create gouts of flame, he says "Incendium!" If it is words, does it even matter the language, or is magic fickle and prefers one language over another?

Magic, voodoo, curses, wizardry, magecraft, spellcraft, witchcraft, mumbo jumbo, or whatever you deem it to be, is just fantasy and wishful thinking. Magic itself requires a god to exist, if only one. If we suppose even a single god does exist we must also suppose this god is the source for magic. It cannot be God, for God Himself states in the Bible that all witches, seers, fortunetellers and magic users are to be put to death. These demands are in books such as Leviticus, Deuteronomy and others. It is paradoxical that God created magic if was not to be used. It could be argued that it is our free will to use magic or not use magic, but it still makes very little sense for an omniscient creator to create something it did not want ever to be used. According to the Bible, God would have you believe that magic—a force in the universe He created—is an abomination, hence the death sentence for using it.

"Here, Billy. I made you a skateboard, but don't you dare ever use it! If you do I will have you killed," could be a usable equivocation. Something more akin to what the Bible says would be, "Here, mankind. I, God, have created an evil force called 'magic'. It is not for you to use, but I am giving it to you anyway. If you do use it, it will mean you will be killed and I will never forgive you, and, oh yes, you will possibly burn forever in a pit of fire, but the decision is yours."

Does that make much sense, especially if I am to be a perfect god? No, of course it does not. From this standpoint, magic seems implausible. From a natural standpoint, it is also a reach to expect that magic is just part of the universal order and that killing a chicken, or mumbling words in any language while making hand gestures, can cause every law of physics, thermodynamics, mathematics and all other areas of science to be momentarily re-written so that something that could never happen will take place.

Voodoo is a widely practiced art, but is it valid? I argue that voodoo is a sugar pill. It is only real to those who believe in it and are in its thrall. Hexes and curses are taken very seriously by millions of people, but what sense is it to actually believe in them? Sticking pins into a straw-and-rag doll can cause another human bodily harm? Ingesting odd mixtures can cure diseases, make people fall in love, or make people hate one another? Killing a bird or a goat while dancing about can cause all sorts of events to take place, such as someone you dislike getting hurt or killed, obtaining a raise or wining a lottery, or even making someone fall in or out of love?

Voodoo priests also claim to be able to create and control zombies, or the living dead. Modern sensibilities tell us that spoken words and powdered substances cannot raise the dead nor can they turn the living into the walking dead…but psychosomatic trauma can certainly have an effect on people. That is what voodoo is; the belief in the magic and its effects are so strong and so fully believed that the voodoo spell is manifested in the subject's/victim's mind. It manifests so strongly that they will act and behave according to what they fear has befallen them. Again, fear is among the easiest of emotions to prey upon. You also have to take into consideration of the education and civilization level of the majority of people who fall for this magic placebo.

No, I am not a bigot or a racist, but a person looking at facts and empirical data. In countries and areas where voodoo and other such magic (like Santeria) are practiced, you have a mainly poor population that is widely uneducated in terms of modern schooling. Many of the people cannot read or write and they are all very religious and superstitious. All it takes is faith to believe the impossible and all it takes is fear to drive superstition. Voodoo and Santeria are mixtures of African superstitions and a belief in black magic mixed with Christianity. You would think that the two are utterly incompatible since the Bible states that magic is evil, anyone who uses it should be put to death and that its use will garner you a nice, comfy spot in Hell.

You also have to factor drugs into all of magic, voodoo, Native American rituals and witchcraft. As far back as ancient times man could derive hallucinogenic compounds from plants and animals. Belladonna, or the flower deadly nightshade for example, was widely used a hallucinogenic material which could be made into ointments. The poison and venom from frogs, toads, salamanders and newts could be used the same way. Plants like the poppy, cannabis, cacti and others have been used by humans to induce altered states. Under the effects of these natural intoxicants all manner of things can be seen and then believed, especially if the substance is introduced unbeknownst to someone—like slipping someone a Mickey.

As much as I like the idea of magic, as cool as casting spells seems to be, it is just not real outside the mind of the believer. Trust me—I read mostly fantasy fiction, I play mostly fantasy games and I love science fiction and fantasy movies and television shows. I would love to ride a flying broomstick, wave a wand and cast fireballs at (certain) people, make some odd hand gestures while speaking in tongues and make people fall in love with me and be able to turn (certain) people into amphibians, but I live in the real world. Magic and miracles are just not part of that world.

Lastly, because I could not think of a better chapter or place to put this next idea, I would like to briefly touch on SHC, or spontaneous human combustion. I say briefly because it is one of the most idiotic notions around and is not deserving of more than a paragraph at best, let alone a chapter or even a book. Living beings do not spontaneously burst into flames, especially ones hot enough to incinerate bone. Even a lightning strike, among the most powerful and heat-producing natural phenomena in the known universe, does not incinerate a living being when it strikes. It will decimate, destroy, burn and char, but never totally incinerates. The human body does not produce enough heat and/or natural chemicals to produce a self-igniting flame intense enough to burn bone to ash. SHC is a myth, a wife's tale and is not real, let alone possible. Like Bigfoot, cases of SHC are attention-craving hoaxes, cases where humans and fire collide (due to either irresponsible behavior or natural means like a lightning strike, an ember from a fireplace…) or are covered-up murders.

Chapter Four: Aliens

Alien visitations, close encounters of the first through fourth kind, alien abductions, ancient astronauts who built some of our world's wonders, lights in the sky, government cover-ups, and secret government bases in the desert…can anyone deny that aliens have and are visiting our little, blue orb?

I do.

Alright; I concede that it is all a possibility. Unlike gods, ghosts and magic, alien visitation is very, very possible. I wholly believe in life on other worlds. Call that life what you will, it undoubtedly exists. The universe is bigger than we can possibly imagine and has been expanding since its inception, or over thirteen billion years. That is thirteen billion years of time for life to evolve on any given planet. By comparison, earth formed roughly nine billion years after the universe came into being and it took a billion or two for life to form on our little rock. That leaves eight to nine billion years for another planet, one that was formed before ours and that turned out to be life-capable, to breed alien life.

Our planet cannot bne unique in that it supports life. Basic mathematics tells us that life exists here on our world and so it exists elsewhere on other worlds. That life may be only lichen on an alien rock wall or it could be humanoid beings. A life-capable planet need not be exactly as earth is; so long as it has water and some sort of atmosphere, life can happen. There is also the possibility of life elsewhere in the universe that is not carbon-based, such as life on earth. It is not impossible for life to exist that is non-carbon based. Our solar system is but one of hundreds of billions of solar systems, so it is inevitable that other planets are out there that support life.

One of the reasons that many devout religious people refuse to acknowledge that life on other planets exists is because to do so brings their religion crashing down all about them. The notion that we humans are divine and special just fades away if the creator of all life made not only us, but also untold other peoples. Who then, are the chosen? Who then, will inherit the kingdom of Heaven or whatever afterlife awaits those of faith? How many messiahs must there be and did they die for alien sins as well? If there is more than one messiah, that too is an uncomforting and demoralizing fact to the faithful. Judaism, Christianity and Islam seem to be incompatible with the prospect of life on other worlds. Just about every other religion is compatible with the possibility, but this is just one reason for the lack of belief in alien life.

Now it is time for me to rant a bit and go into some deep scientific detail about some facts about the universe in which we live. For the people who are unscientific, or who have never studied physics, astrophysics and the science of space, I promise not to be dull and long-winded and I hope you not only find it as severely interesting as I do, but I hope you learn something new and useful as well. Rest assured that the following scientific blabbering will all have a point, but you need to indulge me first.

Okay, ready? Let us start with a few scientific laws that we humans have assigned to the universe. We have assigned these laws because scientists have studied, tested, re-tested, applied and tested yet again principles on how matter/energy reacts to a given set of dynamics on our planet, other planets, and in space. When after hundreds and/or thousands of studies are done, all producing a similar effect/result, a scientific law (usually called a theory) is named.

Before I get too deep into this small and quick science lesson, let me just say that one of the arguments against science that I hear often enough to irk me is this: some people dispute that physics is universal. "How do you know that physics and theories work elsewhere in the universe as they do here?" I want to answer that with a shovel to the head at times, but everyone is allowed to have their doubts. I am no Carl Sagan or Stephen Hawking, not by a long shot, but I know enough. The laws we have assigned to the universe must work the same here as they do one hundred million light years from here. Gravity, for example, is gravity. Whether you are on planet Earth, Mars, Hoth, Alderon, Tatooine, or on Vulcan, gravity works in the same manner. Gravitational forces may be different due to planetary mass, the atmosphere type, the size and elemental make-up of the planet's core, the speed of the planet's rotation, the tilt of its axis and other factors, but gravity will act as we know it. In the vacuum of space, gravity is constant in that there is no gravity, hence why in space an object in motion tends to stay in motion unless an outside force acts upon it. Look at it this way—Earth spins at roughly 17,000 mile per hour on its axis. It has been that way for billions of years, only slowing down after our oceans and then our moon was formed. A full day upon Earth used to be roughly twelve to fourteen hours, but after the oceans and the moon it slowed to the twenty-four hour day we are used to. What keeps our world spinning is that its momentum is perpetual thanks to the law that objects in the vacuum of space stay in motion until an outside force intercedes.

Since outer space is basically one inconceivably big area with no discernible cardinal directions, and we know that the universe is and has been expanding since the dawn of our time, the laws we assign here in our corner of the universe must act the same all over. The speed of light, for example, is a good start. We know that the speed of light is 186,000 miles per second in a vacuum. Can you imagine that? That is fast! Our sun is approximately ninety-three million miles from earth, yet it takes a sunbeam just eight point three minutes to leave the sun and strike our planet. All our studies show that light always travels at the speed of light as far as we can measure it. Why would it be different outside an area that we can measure? What I mean is, would light not travel at 186,000 miles per second somewhere else in space just because it is too far away for us to measure? That is highly unlikely. I weigh one hundred and fifty pounds. Would I weigh less if I found myself on the far side of the universe?

If you were not aware, the light we see at night generated by all the stars is not only beautiful, but it is far away. Almost all of the light from the tiny dots that we see blanketing the night sky may not even have sources any more. The light generated by stars travels at the speed of light, but the stars are so far away that the star itself may have died since that light was generated. It can take light thousands, even millions of years to reach where we are in space—even traveling at the speed of light. Think of it this way: At 186,000 miles per second a beam of light can travel

11,160,000 miles in one earth minute. That is 66,960,000 miles it travels in one hour. In one day it can travel 160,704,000,000 miles. Imagine how far it could travel in a month, a year, a decade, or a century? What about a million years? Imagine something traveling at the speed of light for a million years and still not reaching its destination. The galaxies and systems we can see via super telescopes like the Hubble telescope are desperately far away—hundreds and thousands of light years away! Imagine the ones beyond the eyes of Hubble? Does that give you an inkling to just how expansive our universe is and the staggering amount of mathematics and numbers involved?

Now, one of the properties of traveling at the speed of light is that only light may travel at the speed of light. Physical matter, as in objects not comprised solely of light, start to gain mass as they accelerate. As an object approaches the speed of light it begins to gain mass exponentially and will attain infinite mass at the speed of light. That would be bad, very bad, hence why light can only travel at the speed of light. What does infinite mass mean? Think of it this way. Take an ordinary household item…let us say a phone book. We take the phone book into outer space and we begin to accelerate it. As it gains speed, its mass begins to increase to unimaginable levels. Once the phone book nears the speed of light—not attains the speed of light, but nears it—the phone book will have attained so much mass that it will become infinitely heavy and that one phone book will weigh more than the entire universe weighs. At that point, space itself would begin to fracture, rupture, split apart, collapse in upon itself. A true Armageddon, an end of all we know would take place. That, my friends, is why only light can travel at the speed of light.

You also have the amazing phenomena that time travel, in a sense, is possible if an object could travel at the speed of light. The same phone book, should you immediately accelerate it to the speed of light, would show up in just about the same spot from where it "launched" from because of time-space continuality.

The Star Wars movies—my favorites—fall prey to the impossibility of light-speed and hyper-drive travel. Even with shields at full and inertial dampeners at full, the Millennium Falcon would destroy the known universe should it ever attain the speed of light. Star Trek gets around this fact by switching to warp drive. Unlike the Falcon's hyper-drive, which propels the spaceship to the speed of light, The Enterprise's warp drive does not so much propel the ship itself but warps the space around the ship by varying degrees. By warping space it somehow propels the ship to velocities the Millennium Falcon—the fastest ship in the galaxy—could never even dream to reach. Warping space, or an engine that can attain hyper-light speed, are both very fantastical notions. The energy required to do so would be so vast that a containment area would be larger than the Enterprise's engine room, larger than the entire second Death Star and larger than a planet!

Since we are conveniently speaking of energy, let us now take it into consideration. Just as your car uses gasoline, a spaceship requires energy to fuel its engines and/or reactors. By today's standards and our best scientific calculations and projections, it would take a tremendous amount of energy to propel a spaceship to near, at, or faster than light speeds. When I say tremendous I am talking about off-the charts energy requirements, numbers that boggle the mind. The energy consumed in this feat would be more than our solar system could produce and that is just to propel the ship. In the vacuum of space, an object in motion stays in motion, so our spaceship would need an equal amount of energy just to stop. This is just for one spaceship and one trip. The energy requirements just are not available in the universe for a fleet of spaceships to constantly travel at such speeds, or even to warp space—at least not as far as we know or can project. No, my friends, mankind, as well as an alien species that have attained our level of technology, are relegated to slow space travel. With all that explained I come to one of my favorite talking points as to why I do not believe in alien visitation.

Lights in the sky—most every unidentified flying object (UFO) or alien sighting story identifies lights in the sky, or strange air/space ships that fly in formation and that are brightly-lit with varying types of lights. Let me ask you one simple question: If a race of beings has the technology to create a vessel that can traverse not only space, but possibly time by warping space at light or faster-than-light speeds and has acquired the level of technology to produce the staggering amount of energy to do so, *do their ships need landing lights?*

When I recently explained this to one of my closest friends, he was very upset. He said that he could not disagree and that I had ruined an old experience he was carrying with him. He never spoke about it as far as I can remember, but he must have seen some lights in the sky one night. With this revelation he concluded he was mistaken in what he saw and that my conclusion made more sense than his own.

Landing lights? Really? A race of people can build a star-spanning ship that can harness an energy source so vast that it rivals the energy requirements of a whole galaxy, but they need lights by which to land? Even our paltry science gives our military vehicles, commandos and police forces radar, sonar and night vision. You would think that a starship would have at least such technology, if not something a hundred times more efficient. And lights? Such gaudy, incriminating lights are necessary to what degree? I would think that, like our stealth planes, any alien ship would have the equipment to cloak itself from detection against our meager capabilities, and colorful lights, or the tell-tale glow produced by reflecting lights from below would be nullified by such a ship.

When people see lights in the sky the only possibility in my mind is that they are mistaken. They are not crazy, just mistaken. I count myself as one of them, for about fourteen years ago my wife and I were witness to something very odd. We were newly married and in that summer we were standing on the deck of our new home. It was night, and as we gazed up into the sky one of us spotted something. It was so high up that it appeared to be where the stars were. This tiny white dot moved in a straight line so fast it was amazing. Then it just stopped and changed direction as if it were a toy in a child's hand, not a vessel slowing, banking and then changing direction. It did this a few times and then it was gone. I can still see it happening in my mind today, but even then I was skeptical.

I wholly believe in life on other planets. I believe that alien races that are at least as smart as we are must exist, but I do not buy that they are secretly playing games in our atmosphere. Skeptical or not, the one thing I fully believe is that when people all over our globe see strange lights and shapes in the sky what they are seeing are military aircraft. Some may be jets and copters of rival agencies, secret agencies, or even the testing of new technology. What better way to test a new stealth type aircraft, or a new form of propulsion then out in the public when the public is known to jump to other-worldly conclusions. Sometimes the best way to hide is right out in the open. What of Area 51? I try not to dwell on government cover-ups and conspiracies. Where there is smoke there is fire, of that I agree. Is Area 51 simply a military base where new technology is tested? That is what I choose to believe. Did an alien space craft crash here on Earth in the desert of the South West? Despite my aversions to believe so, nothing is impossible—highly improbable, but not impossible. It is within reason that there is an alien race capable of star-spanning capability. Perhaps they use light-speed or faster-than-light travel, or perhaps they traverse space at a much slower, more economic and realistic way. It is possible that such an alien ship, maybe a scout ship or recon ship from a larger and far-off mother ship, could have run into problems while in our sector of the universe and saw us as any port in a storm. That is what could be in Area 51; the remains of the crash. I do not buy it, but it is possible.

For the rest of this chapter let us assume that there are one or more races of aliens who have and still visit our world. There are many things that need to be brought to light if indeed we are being visited. First is that how many races are involved in this situation? Almost every ancient culture either claims, or tacitly implies, some sort of alien visitation or sighting. Most of these ancient accounts are all recorded as benign occurrences. Many claim that these visitations resulted in the construction of great monuments where aliens either built, or helped to build, enduring structures, as with the great pyramids of Egypt, Mexico and Pan and South America, and also the statues on Easter Island—that is what we call the Ancient Astronaut theory.

It is only in modern times that alien visitation is usually considered a harbinger of death and doom, or with insidious intent like abduction, to study and dissect and study us. Again, my own little theory makes the most sense. A race of beings that has the knowhow and technology to craft star-spanning ships, that can build such advanced engines that can reach incalculable speeds, while not consuming more energy than a galaxy can provide and have a civilization thousands—or hundreds of thousands—of years ahead of our own would certainly know biology. When a race is advanced to the point that they can travel the stars, I like to think they know what an eye does, know what a stomach is for and know what other body parts and functions are for. If they do not then something is wrong with the entire picture.

Even if alien beings did want to dissect us and study us, you would think they did so eons ago if and when they first visited Earth. Why would they still need to abduct humans today? If they wished continual studies it would be astronomically more efficient to have kept our predecessors from previous visits as slaves for breeding purposes, but that suggests all aliens are cruel and indifferent. In this scenario, if they are, it would be easier to clone us, for if they can warp space or travel faster-than-light, they can clone a human.

I propose that alien races who are advanced enough to travel the universe are dissecting no other sentient beings. We humans, as smart and as clever as we are, are the true dimwits of the cosmos. We are the ones who want to kill, dissect, enslave and control everything that crosses our path. If, a thousand years from now, we start spanning the stars, we are the race most likely to abduct other life forms and dissect them in the name of science.

On to the theory of ancient astronauts we go! Let us say that mankind has indeed been visited by an alien race advanced enough to get to Earth. These alien travelers came upon our world and decided to pay us a visit. They could tell long before they had arrived that the state of technology and civilization at the time was at the bottom of the totem pole. We must assume, in any case of ancient astronauts, that the aliens were benign and did not wish us any harm. We assume this because, if the theory is true, they helped us build great structures, or at least set us on the path to do so. My query is why did they do this? To what end and what did it hope to accomplish? If advanced beings landed and either built us, or helped us to build, great structures, why were they made of stone? Yes, stone can last thousands of years where metal or iron would rust and decay. Would not these aliens show us how to smelt things more advanced than bronze, copper and gold? Would they not teach us to smelt and create iron, steel, or mixtures of elements to make superior, long-lasting structures? Would the buildings not be more futuristic and less archaic like a pyramid?

Whether in Egypt, South America, or wherever ancient cities lay that claim some sort of ancient astronaut story, why do we not find evidence of more advanced design? By advanced design I mean things like non-fire lighting, elevators—why not teleport pads?—heating/air conditioning systems, running water and so forth? Please do not get me wrong; I give full and amazing credit to the ancients who built all those pyramids, temples, cities, statutes and so forth. Their craftiness and style have yet to be truly understood and are so steeped in mystery that some people can only come to the conclusion that an outside force must have been involved. Why would a star-spanning race come across the universe to help us build stone structures? It only makes sense that they would impart their genius upon us, even if we were too immature a species to learn all of it. Were, then, these ancient astronauts naught but bored galactic philanthropists? Did it please them to scour the universe for signs of planets with intelligent life that was early into its development and then go play in the dirt with them and build great buildings and then leave…never to be heard from again?

That sounds ridiculous, of course, but is it possible? What of the Nazca lines, or English crop circles? Are those not tell-tale signs that we have been visited and we await the return of our alien allies? Well, crop circles I do not want to get into, because those are pure man-made foolishness. It is a fine hobby, with talented artists doing the work, but it is no great mystery worth delving into, at least not in my opinion. The Nazca lines, however, are worth talking about.

Without going into great detail for those who know what the Nazca lines are…in Peru, ancient natives made etchings in the earth that were very large. They chose animals, and etched spiders, monkeys, sharks, lizards, and other animal shapes into the plateaus. There are also human-like etchings. Some of these etchings measure more than six-hundred feet across and can be seen from very high up in the sky. The ancient Peruvian Indians could not fly, however, so why etch these pictograms into the earth? Were they not trying to communicate with aliens who had visited, or had been visiting, our world? Were they showing the aliens where to land when next they came? I do not buy into that line of theory and I try and use the smarts I possess to tell me otherwise.

The etchings were of the animals the Peruvians lived with, hunted, ate, kept as pets and saw all around. Why on Earth would they etch them to impress an alien race? Why, too, would they draw animals and not images of the aliens, or their space craft? To me, the lines drawn by the Nazca are amazing feats of creativity and they do have their origins in the heavens, but not for alien visitors. I am thinking higher up the food chain; gods. The pagan Peruvians paid homage to many gods and most ancient American-Indian cultures revered animal-gods. In North America, many natives believed that the crow, coyote, bear and lion were all gods, as were the sun, the moon and the stars. The native Peruvians would and did anthropomorphize (the assigning of human traits to animals and objects and also an act of assigning animals god-like stature) the animals in their own environment. Perhaps the etchings were to please and/or appease their gods. Perhaps they were rituals to bring forth rain, or a bountiful crop-growing season, or to secure good hunting. Who knows what these ancients were thinking, for they left no notes or written history. It is all quite possible that an ancient Peruvian king or tribal ruler was eccentric and had the lines etched to appease his own creative or dream-inspired whims.

One of the most remote places on our planet is Easter Island, a small island in the southeastern Pacific Ocean and part of the Polynesian Islands. Centuries ago a once-mighty tribal nation reigned on the beautiful, lush land mass. The people of the area, the Rapanui, ruled the island and made it famous for two reasons. The most famous are the 887 statutes called moai. These moai are huge carvings of humanoid heads and upper torsos, hewn out of a stone called tuff, a very hard condensed volcanic ash. Other moai are carved from basalt, another strong stone. The 887 statues feature predominantly large heads, nearly all three-fifths as large in comparison to the body of the statue. The faces are all emotionless, with a proud, enigmatic if not monotonous cast to them, with jutting chins, thin mouths and large, long, angular yet flat noses. All the moai are dated to between 1200 A.D. to 1500 A.D; not so long ago in the grand scope of human civilization. What did it take for the natives to carve such descriptive statues? What tools were at their disposal and what happened to them? How did these uncivilized, secluded, island-dwelling people hew such massive stones from the far-off quarries and transport them across the island? Why is there no record of how they did all this? The why is simple; the Rapanui had no written history, much like all native Indian cultures. They left no clues other than their artwork.

The second reason the Rapanui are famous is because of what they did to their island, and ultimately to themselves. They raped the island of every known resource and over the centuries were a starving, warring people. What was once a lush paradise of an island was soon turned into a rocky, barren wasteland devoid of anything, save for mountains and huge stone statues. After the last fruit was eaten, the last animal was hunted and the last tree cut down, all that was left was to turn to war and cannibalism to survive—but no one did survive. It must have been a horrific end, and the moai are not talking.

Were the moai likenesses of alien visitors? Did ancient astronauts give these people the tools for which to carve and move these great, massive stone statues? If so, what happened to those tools and machines? Were the tools used to expertly carve hard rocks on loan by the visitors and were then collected when the Rapanui were done with their work, or after they had all died off? Highly unlikely.

The last subject on the ancient astronaut theory I would like to discuss is of the antediluvian Bolivian site of Puma Punku. Estimated to be built between 200 B.C and 500 A.D., Puma Punka, or Gate of the Panther, was erected on the shores of what was Lake Titicaca, where it was in the Andes. The gate, the walls around it, and monoliths nearby are a mystery; no one knows how the Bolivian Indians managed to not only get the huge and massively heavy hewn stones to the site, but also how they carved them. The walls were made of inter-locking stones that were not only large, but also beautifully decorated with carvings. The area, now a ruin, was once a marvel of architecture and art. The stones were said to have fit so perfectly together, so seamlessly laid, that the Bolivians at the time had neither the tools nor the know how to create such a wonder. Many agree that even by today's standards, with our wondrous tools, technology and ingenuity that modern man could barely make a structure half as well as did the ancient Bolivians. Their crude stone tools were not meant for the precision cuts and shaping of the near-diamond hard rock that was used to make Puma Punku. Their only means of water transport were reed rafts and boats, so how was it all done? At more than 12,000 feet above sea level, it is impossible to say how the stones arrived. Par for the course is that these ancient people left us no written history by the time they had vanished or had been killed off by European/Mediterranean invaders.

Did an alien race help them move the stones? Did an alien race give them the tools for which to create the Panther's Gate? If so, why and to what end? Where are the remnants of these tools? Would not one be unearthed over the centuries? Why is it that all over the world, wherever monolithic stones are and ancient runes lay, that we assume the ancient peoples could not have built them on their own? People always say the ancients were so wise, yet we need to believe aliens had to have a hand in the construction of stone marvels? There is no record of how and why people all over the ancient world, from different time periods, built or carved archaic structures. Modern people can only assume and hypothesize as to the why and the how, but that is what drives anthropologists and archeologists—the quest for the how and the why. How were these structures built? What was the inspiration behind them? How were massive stones, weighing more tons than was feasible to move at that point in history, moved to remote locations? Even today with our superior intelligence can we not figure out how these more primitive peoples moved such stones and were able to cut and craft them? Why, I ask again, does it have to be aliens?

It makes more sense to me that these ancient people were craftier than we give them credit for. All over the ancient world peoples were hewing massive stones from mountains and quarries and moving them; from England to Africa, the Middle East to Bolivia and Peru to Mexico and Chile. They are in Russia, Rome, Europe and Asia. All over the globe, as far back as mankind has recorded his own history, monolithic statues and huge walls and temples were built. Someone knew the secrets. Did aliens visit every culture (at different times during human history) just to move stones and build temples and walls for us? Did they come just to let us borrow amazing tools only to take them back when were done toiling with tons of the hardest stones on the planet? If so, was it just one race of aliens, or were there other alien cultures that were competing for the Good Citizen of the Galaxy award?

I cannot prescribe to any of that. It is much more likely that humans figured out how to move, carve, and shape monolithic stones on their own and each culture did so in a way that worked for them. The same goes for the carving of the stones. It is also more likely that one or more ancient cultures found the secret and it was passed on from culture-to-culture somehow without ever being physically recorded. Perhaps traveling traders, or travelling emissaries took the knowledge from culture-to-culture, or these methods could have even been sold as intellectual property.

The principle of Occam's razor, or "all things being equal the simplest solution is the best one", seems to fit very well here.

How do you explain that there are pyramids in Egypt and pyramids in South America? There are also ones in far eastern countries. These cultures were unaware of each other until modern times, so how do you explain the same sort of structure appearing all over the ancient world? I am glad you asked.

In regards to how ancient man had figured out how to hew and move enormous stones, I like to compare pyramids and like structures to biology. How so? There is a little thing biologists call Convergent Evolution. Just as birds, bats and insects—all separate animal species, separated by different time periods of when they evolved—all developed wings, so too did ancient man develop his ancient cities. The wing, something bats, birds and insects found advantageous, ancient man figured out that one of the strongest shapes in nature was a three-sided structure. Round or square was a good, sturdy shape for a smaller building, but it was easier to build up in the shape of a triangle. The building used fewer components and was structurally stronger. It is logical that man would start to build convergent structures as his architectural capacity increased. Just as animals evolved with convergence, so too did humankind's architectural skills evolve. That is the way I see it, in the least. It makes more sense than believing an alien race came here for no better reason than to play building blocks with an ancient alien (to them) race.

Are we alone? I highly doubt it. If there are races on other planets that are advanced enough to travel the immense span of the universe, how many are there? Mathematics says it has to be more than one, but is it two, a dozen, a hundred, more? Irrevocably if they exist they must know of each other to some degree. If so, how do they tend to visitations of Earth and other planets? Do they have some creed like in Star Trek? Trekkies all know of the Prime Directive, the cardinal law of The Federation of Planets; in a nut shell, do not get involved or interfere with the development of a lesser civilization. If something like that is real, do alien societies share that view? If mathematics is wrong and we are the most advanced species in the universe, then it may well be mankind will never meet another sentient race, for the science that would have us travel the stars to meet other life resides only within books and on the silver screen. I say that because of the things I fully *do* believe is that our species will implode and destroy itself—if not our own planet—long before we develop the science necessary to carry us to the far reaches of the universe.

Chapter Five: Bigfoot

Bigfoot. Sasquatch. Yeti. Yowie. Grey Man. Every nation has its own version of a large, hairy, ape-like humanoid that runs amok in the wilderness, is seldom seen and never caught. As with ghosts, all we have for proof are grainy photos, poorly-shot video, many plaster casts of feet impressions and some hair that people claim is neither animal nor human. We also have lots and lots of hoaxes. There is no concrete proof of a Bigfoot, just faith. Not to rain on anyone's parade out of malice, but here is another mystery that is just silly to an educated person, yet so many educated people (many much smarter than humble me) believe an ape-man is out there somewhere. In order to understand the smoke behind the fire, we must travel back into pre-history and to the origins of humans.

Long before we were *homo-sapiens*, what we are today, our ancestors were apes. All egos aside, we were apes. Get over yourself, your ego, your upbringing and your religious dogmas if you need to, and if believe otherwise that is fine. The one thing that is not theory but fact is the evolution of the species. The beauty of science, of evidence, and of facts is that they do not require that you believe in them. They are what they are; they do not lie, have no agenda, and do not care what religion says about them. Facts are just facts, and sometimes the truth hurts, but not maliciously.

From out Africa all those eons ago we came, and we spread out over Asia and the European continent. Humans have gone through millions of years and hundreds of species changes to get where we are today, and along the way a long-lost cousin must have spawned the Bigfoot myth.

Gigantopithecus was an ancestor of ours that lived in parts of Asia, mainly China and India, one million years ago and went extinct about three-hundred thousand to one-hundred thousand years ago. This more ape than man is the largest ape on record, topping the charts at more than nine-feet tall and weighing over a thousand pounds. Other large apes, as well as hominids, have been found world-wide, but this guy was the largest. Hominids were ape-like creatures that showed signs of development toward modern-day humans, but were still more animal than human. They shared our upright posture, bi-pedal locomotion, could use and fashion primitive tools and lived in family-style troops. *Gigantopithecus* fossils show a large, strong, cold-adapted hominid with a somewhat pointed skull. There is debate over if it was bi-pedal or not, but many favor a bi-pedal creature since it's skull seems to suggest a wide lower jaw supported by a thick windpipe, which is evidence of a fully erect spinal column. It is possible that a few hundred (or less) *Gigantopithecus* survived into an era where modern humans existed in parts of China and India where most of these legends have their origin. When I say modern, I mean seven to ten thousand years ago, when humans were at a point where they could observe and record history and could possibly have come across these creatures. Another likelihood is that modern day humans of ancient times came across the bones of these long-extinct creatures and made monsters out of them, considering them giants, titans, Cyclops and other creatures of lore.

Asia was not the only home to large apes and hominids for they spread across the globe and adapted to the regions they had settled into. Evolution and the survival of the fittest took its toll on all the hominids and soon *homo-erectus* appeared on the scene. By this time, most hominid species had gone the way of the dodo and were extinct. It is certain that the hardier ones hung on longer, but by the time one of the last few great ice ages came about and only Cro-Magnon man and modern *homo-sapiens* were left to vie for the planet, the hominids were gone, *Gigantopithecus* included.

Or were they? Modern-day Bigfoot believers suggest that hominids did not die out and that more than one species survives to this very day. If so, they are among the most intelligent, resilient, cunning and elusive creatures on the planet. To have avoided detection and extinction all this time makes them the ultimate survivalists. Forget the CIA, FBI, Navy seals, Green Berets and Army Rangers because these Bigfoot, yeti and yowie beat them all when it comes to covert ops. No one has been able to catch one alive or bring in the carcass of one. No one has a true, valid, decently pixilated photograph of one. No one has any bones that have not been deemed fake or that are not an animal we cannot identify. Just like with ghosts, all the evidence we have for a Bigfoot is shaky at best, definitely hearsay and if it were valid this chapter would not be in this book.

Let us begin with what we do not have. We do not have a body, alive or dead. After thousands of years of people supposedly sighting, or encountering this creature, we have yet to capture a live Bigfoot on camera or in the flesh. We do not have the corpse of a Bigfoot that has not been ruled a hoax, nor do we have any skeletons of their dead. All we do have is hearsay reports, people all over the world wanting fifteen minutes of fame for their hoaxes, plaster casts of feet and some odd hairs that are most likely hoaxes as well.

What we do know of ape and human behavior certainly fits into the Bigfoot myth. By all reports a Bigfoot is less a man and more an ape. As such it would have ape intelligence, which is considerable for an animal but pales in comparison to human intelligence. Bigfoot must be treated as either an ape or a modern-day hominid. In either case its intelligence is sub-human. How then, does it elude us persistently? As either an ape or a hominid, a Bigfoot has to be a foraging omnivore; it could be a predatory creature, but that does not fit with an ape or a hominid. Yes, yes, some chimpanzees often hunt monkeys and such, but those are social hunts done in broad daylight and are less for the meat and more for the kill and for rank and dominance displays. Of the great apes none are known to hunt for food. Even the largest of silver-backed mountain gorillas hunt only bamboo and tubers.

A Bigfoot would most likely be like the extinct giant ground sloths of pre-ice age times. They would be mainly herbivorous but not opposed to scavenging the remains of a deceased animal, or chasing a smaller predator off a kill. What would their food source be? In the pine forests of North West America it would be leaves, berries, nuts and carrion—not unlike a grizzly bear. In the mountains of Nepal where these creatures are called Yeti, food becomes more of a problem. The cold, inhospitable terrain at high altitudes allows for little vegetation to grow and the mountain goats that eke out a life have a hard time finding food. Food, however, would not be the biggest problem for Bigfoot.

Where there is one Bigfoot there has to be more. Hominids were social creatures. Apes and humans are social creatures. Not only do we need to live in some sort of troop or society, we need to breed. Not only do we need to breed, but we need to breed with members not directly related to us so we do not muck up the gene pool. Just as lions, wolves, bears, badgers, beavers, birds and ape males leave their birth territory to seek new lands and new members of their own species, a Bigfoot would need to do the same. It makes zero sense that there are just a few Bigfoot in every pocket of the world where they are reported to be found and that these tiny clusters of creatures routinely mate with each other to produce the next generation. For starters the whole clan would be long deceased due to horribly-defected gene pools—each generation would be born more deformed than the last, easily prone to sickness and malformation. Most obvious is that these creatures would just not have the brain power to come to the conclusion that the only way to survive is to limit their numbers and breed only with their next of kin.

From our caveman days up through today, humans have set out on journeys to meet fresh mates. Even the American Indians would have large gatherings where members of similar tribes (and at times just friendly tribes) would gather to trade, celebrate, and meet new mates. The same would have to hold true for hominids like Bigfoot. With no genetic diversity the entire race would succumb to nature's apathetic grip.

Next, where would a Bigfoot or a yeti live? They do not live like any other ape lives, which is out in the open. If that were the case this chapter would not be in this book. The only other alternative is that all Bigfoot and yeti instinctively seek out massive cave systems and have an underground network of tunnels. Is there any other way for huge ape-men to live in such remote and/or inhospitable environments? Why have we never found such caves? How intelligent must a Bigfoot be to seclude itself in such a cave and only venture forth to eat? As far as I know no caves systems have been found anywhere in the world that show evidence of a large hominid species living within it. No primitive tools have been found, no carcasses of any carrion, or prey it might ingest, have been found with ape-like or hominid teeth marks. No caves have been found that bear the bodies of dead Bigfoot. They have to live somewhere.

No bears, wolves, or mountain lion (or snow leopard dens in the case of the yeti) have been found containing the carcasses or skeletons of a Bigfoot, nor is there such an animal on record to be found with tell-tale ape/hominid tooth marks on its body or in its bones to show evidence of struggles or predation. Where do Bigfoot put their dead and what do they do with them? After thousands of years there should be some stockpile of bones or bodies, unless the believers would have us swallow that Bigfoot are far too intelligent and do something with the bodies of their dead that belies human detection and ability to find.

The only conclusion is that Bigfoot is just a myth. Perhaps it has roots in reality if a hominid species was able to persevere into an era when men had begun carving out their own civilizations. The two species could have come across one another many thousands of years ago and no one would be able to deny it.

The true reality is that hominids are extinct and if any were alive today humans would have encountered them, as we do all other forest animals of such size. We do not live in Tarzan-like days, or in Lewis and Clark times where there are huge creatures that exist and we do not know of them. There are indeed a multitude of plants and animals we do not know of yet, but these specimens are always small lizards, birds, insects, or tree-dwelling animals that are smaller than the average lap dog. The forests of the American North West and the mountains of Nepal are not the deep, mysterious oceans where elusive and undiscovered creatures await our ever-seeking eyes. Now that I have my segue let us move on to the next mystery.

Chapter Six: Lake Monsters

New England has Champ of Lake Champlain. Canada's Lake Okanagan has Ogopogo. Africa's Congo boasts Mokele-mbembe. The most famous, of course, is Nessie of Loch Ness in Scotland. Across the world almost every nation claims to have a fresh water lake inhabited by a monster. Loch Ness may be one of the few saltwater claims, making it even more fantastic. Why am I so skeptical? Why do I not believe the hundreds of eye-witnesses and testimonies? Thanks for asking! Growing up I had three loves—no, not Charlie's Angels, though I was always partial to Kate Jackson and definitely Tanya Roberts. I loved dinosaurs, I loved mythology and I loved comic book superheroes. As I grew older, I studied all three intently. For the longest time I wanted to be a paleontologist, but learned that I hated sand and digging in the dirt, especially under a hot sun (thanks to trips to the beach) and so I left my dreams of unearthing dinosaur bones for just reading and learning about the ancient beasts. All through my life I have tried to keep current with the latest news and discoveries in the paleontological world.

When you know enough about dinosaurs and other ancient creatures the less you believe in lake monsters. Hundreds of millions of years ago, after the seas were teeming with marine life creatures had begun to leave the Earth's massive oceans for dry land. The first to evolve were the amphibians, but they were not the smallish creatures we know today. Many of these were large, toothy predators who could kill a man and swallow them whole. Eventually many amphibians evolved further and became reptiles. Before even the smallest dinosaur walked the Earth reptiles were the ruling class. After millions of more years of trials, tribulations and changes, dinosaurs appeared. During those years, however, many reptiles found themselves returning to the seas in search for food. It is a scenario that would play out once more many millions of years later when mammals had evolved and a few species returned to the oceans and became whales, dolphins, seals and walrus.

By the time dinosaurs were ruling the land, colossal reptiles ruled the seas. Many people who are into dinosaurs love the popular and mighty tyrannosaurs rex, or the deadly and agile velociraptor, or the armored tanks that were the stegosaurs, ankylosaurs, or the triceratops. I was always partial to the sea-going reptiles, which were not dinosaurs but ancient marine reptiles of unthinkable power. Many of these reptiles grew to enormous proportions and would make T-Rex look like a wolf as compared to a lion. There were nothrosaurs, pilosaurs, plesiosaurs, ichthyosaurs, crocodilians and more. There was one crocodile, deinosuchus, so big that it grew to almost fifty-feet long and could eat pretty much anything it wanted. Deinosuchus's sea-going cousins were no slouches and some grew as large as modern-day whales and had huge heads with mouths that were no joke. T-rex was the bad boy of dinosaurs with its head that could be almost four-feet long and its six to eight-inch teeth. Marine reptiles, mostly the giant pilosaurs like kronosaurus and liopleurodon, could grow to forty to fifty-feet or more and had heads that could be up to twelve-feet long and filled with giant teeth. If any of these animals interests you, I suggest doing some simple library or online research into these ancient reptiles—it is simply amazing what creatures nature has produced.

Since all these reptiles are extinct, save for deinosuchus's smaller cousins—alligators, crocodiles and caiman—we base what we know of them by looking at their bones and studying living reptiles. What we do know tells us this: reptiles are cold-blooded animals that need the sun to help maintain their body temperature. Reptiles are mostly carnivorous with very, very few of them being vegetarians. Reptiles reproduce by laying eggs out of the water buried in sand and/or dirt. There are a rare few reptile species that give birth to live young, but these are not marine dwellers.

There are also things we know about our planet's past by studying both paleontology and geology. The continents have been moving and shifting since our planet was formed. When we look at maps and globes we see the familiar shape of the world in geographic terms, but the land masses all started out as one huge mass (named Pangaea) and have been separating, colliding, separating again and moving since their inception. As such, the oceans we know now were not the same. There were still huge, deep abysses but there were many shallow seas as well as land-locked seas. The temperature of the world during the time of the ancient reptiles and dinosaurs was higher than it is now, making the seas and the shallow seas much warmer than they are today. Those warm seas helped the marine reptiles to thrive since they could hunt with more energy and worry less about freezing to death in cold waters. Unlike mammals, reptiles do not have layers of blubber to insulate them against the cold. The ancient world and its seas were warm and the reptiles would not have needed blubber, and so never evolved it as a defense against the cold.

Reptiles, however, did evolve the world's most magnificent form of insulation, feathers! I say that with my lip bit because I am among those that fully, truly, honestly believe that dinosaurs were not reptiles, but had evolved into warm-blooded animals. I am not going on fait—never that—but all the studies of the brilliant paleontologists that have spent decades working on, studying, and pouring over fossils. Call the dinosaurs warm-blooded reptiles if you will, but it was the dinosaurs that evolved feathers and it was the smaller theropod dinosaurs that evolved/changed into birds. It is no secret that your barnyard chicken, Tom Turkey, the annoying city slicker pigeons and the mighty bald eagle are the descendants of T-rex and its kin.

Why this history/dinosaur lesson? It is all relative to marine reptiles. For even a single species of marine reptile to have survived all the extinctions ancient animals have gone through, including more than several ice ages since their demise, would be one of the greatest miracles of nature. Even if this slimmest of slim, minutest, craziest chance took place, the odds against continued survival without human detection seals the deal as to why lake and sea monsters (that are reptiles) do not exist.

The oceans and seas of today, even the shallower ones, are just too cold to support large sea-going reptiles. Even fresh water lakes get too cold in winter time to harbor a marine reptile. Take alligators, crocodiles, and caiman as an example; they do not inhabit the open oceans, and only dwell where the water is warm. Australian salt-water crocodiles occasionally venture out into the sea, but it is for quick trips to other river systems, and not to stay. Is it possible that a marine reptile from many millions of years ago could have survived and adapted to cold water, or to a cold environment? Turtles have colonized most of the inhabited world and manage to last through winter just fine, but a large predatory water-dweller with no hands/feet/claws would not be able to hibernate in the ground like a turtle does.

It is not known if any of ancient marine reptiles were able to give birth to live young, but taking clues from every known study of the fossil record and judging by today's reptiles it seems that there were egg layers. That would entail them having to come ashore to nest. A lake monster has to breed to survive. As I argued with Bigfoot, are we to assume that aside from being masters of eluding modern science that they are smart enough to limit themselves to just a few at a time so that they can continue to exist without alerting us pesky humans? Ridiculous! There needs to be more than one monster in a lake for it to breed, that is obvious. There needs to be a colony of these things to be able to breed, for females of every species are picky and only choose the male most suited to pass along his genes. They do not pick the first tall, dark and toothy male that courts them. Tell me how a colony of large, air-breathing animals eludes man and science for so long.

The most popular marine reptile is the plesiosaur, made famous by the Loch Ness monster. This species of ancient marine reptile could grow up to forty-feet long and had a long neck akin to a giraffe's that was as long as its body was…or more. A small head topped the neck, usually filled with long, needle-like teeth. It is supposed that the stiff-necked plesiosaurs swam through the water and swung its head from side-to-side through schools of fish and other smaller sea life and used its long teeth to snare food. Plesiosaurs, with their small heads, had the brain the size of a small fruit (if they were lucky), so it is impossible for them to be able to outsmart man.

The theory of underwater caves and grottos does not hold any water, all pun intended, for the creatures need fresh air and would still have to find a way to sun themselves for hours each day. Just like George

Hamilton and loads of beach goers, reptiles need to catch a few hours of rays each day to get their metabolism started and so they do not freeze to death. They cannot do this in water and so must spend an hour or two each morning sunning themselves to provide them with enough energy to power their body's syatems. Where are these areas? Why has no one seen a basking reptile?

These predators would also need to roam open waters looking for food, mates and a place to nest. If they roam they would be seen! Run silent, run deep does not apply to an air-breather. Where are the creatures? Where are their skeletons and the rotting carcasses of the deceased? In each case of a lake monster it is always just one monster per lake that is sighted, so are the believers saying that these creatures are quasi-immortal and just never die? It must be for we have never seen signs of nests, eggs, young, or hatchery areas where the young are reared. There are none because these creatures no longer exist.

As with our friend Bigfoot, there is no proof for lake monsters. If the believers have to offer are hearsay statements, grainy photographs, or amateur video showing ripples from far away, you have nothing to stand on. We have the technology to spy on people from outer space but not to catch an air-breathing, twenty to fifty-foot creature on camera, radar, or sonar?

"Alright, Captain Skeptical, what if these lake monsters are all fish and not reptiles?" Well, every report is of a reptilian-like creature, with a long, flexible neck, some sort of finless tail and flippers. Fish have fins, not flippers. No fish to date has a long, flexible neck. Eels are slim-lined creatures with no real neck, so do not try the giant eel routine. Moreover, fish have not grown to such super size since the times when reptiles ruled the seas and mammals were not even beginning to evolve. There are fish in the fossil record that have reached colossal size, like *dunkleosteus,* which could reach thirty-three feet in length. The mammoth megalodon was a shark just like the great white of today, except this monster grew to almost seventy-feet long and had jaws big enough that could swallow a rowboat full of sailors. Imagine what that beast could have done at Amnity Island! There are even bigger fish still found in the fossil record, but none had the characteristics assigned to any "known" lake monster. The only fish with a neck remotely flexible is the seahorse, but I doubt those cute, tiny and benign creatures are the ones haunting our world's lakes.

The only lake monsters out there are alligators and crocs, anacondas and pythons and the human pirates that still roam certain areas of our oceans. While it is fun to think an ancient sea monster can still roam our lakes and lochs it's just not supported by enough facts and it defies everything we know about nature. The believers can believe all they like and the skeptics (like me) can try and persuade people otherwise, but at the end of the day there is no definitive proof.

Chapter Seven: Vampires & Werewolves

The two most famous movie monsters have to be Dracula and the Wolf-man. Actors Bela Lugosi and Lon Channey made these nasties of the night big hits, but there are those who truly believe in the undead (or living dead, as some like to call them) and shape-shifters. Human beings, for all our intelligence, will believe just about anything. If there is a universe full of intelligent life, we Earth-men and women must be among the most gullible creatures ever to exist. We routinely believe in absurdities of every kind and let our fears and emotions rule out over every scrap of wisdom, science and common sense.

Remember how in the last chapter I had said that mythology was one of my passions? Well, I include monsters as part of mythology. Every culture has their monsters, including some sort of ghoul or undead to shape-shifters, and I began reading about and studying them in elementary school. I have also written six other books, all fantasy fiction novels (under a nome de plume). While I may not believe in gods, magic, the undead, or were-creatures, I sincerely love crafting stories about all of it.

We shall begin with vampires, the most popular of monsters ever to be created. Although Bram Stoker, who wrote *Dracula in* 1897 and made the living dead immensely popular, myths of vampires and like creatures date back much, much further. The word vampire in its current form is a derivative of many languages, mainly German, French and Slavic. From *upir* to wampir, from to *vampir* and *vamprye* it is not far to reach vampire. A quick observation of the old Slavic world, especially Albania where many of the myths began, is the old words in Albanian for teeth/fangs and sucking: dhamb (da-am) for fang sand pire (peer) for the verb sucking. Dahmb-pire…vampire. Keep in mind that the English language is not a romance language, meaning it is not Latin-based. English is a Gothic-based language and is of Eastern European Germanic-Gothic influence.

Tales of vampires as demons and evil creatures started floating around as early as the Mesopotamians and ancient Hebrews, as well as in ancient Greece, Persia and Russia. China's mythology tells of flesh-eating, blood-drinking creatures that were demons. In my opinion I see the process of evolution in all things, not just the species. Animals evolve, relationships evolve, religions evolve and mythology and tall-tales evolve. I believe the vampire myth evolved from the act of cannibalism.

In pre-historic times cannibalism may have been looked at and treated much differently, even to early *homo-sapiens*. By the time our cultural and societal values evolved, mankind looked at cannibalism differently and the act became garish, ghoulish, inhumane and ultimately the act of a demonic being. Mankind is wonderful at making not only gods, but at making monsters. We humans hate seeing the bad in ourselves and so we project the bad and the evil into beings and creatures that do not really exist…but we make them exist and fashion them into our religions and worst nightmares.

Today we see vampires in a different way; they are powerful, immortal, even romantic beings capable of a wide array of human emotions and possessing a wide array of wants and desires. We have romanticized vampires so much that now they are movie heroes, video games and a best-selling young fiction series. Ancient tales of vampires told of demons and demon spirits that ate flesh and drank blood. These tales, dating back to a time when humans first began to record history, could only be taken further. As man progressed through the ages, so did his fantastic tales, as well as his ability to demonize his fellow man. Anyone that was different, un-liked, or perhaps a bad seed, could be labeled a demon. People of rival villages or rival nations were easily demonized. People of a different religion were easily demonized. Humans are the kings and queens of hate. Statically it is religion that fuels most all of the hatred known in the world, but it also fuels and is fueled by it as well. The same holds true for fear. There are such glorious (I say facetiously) escapades as the Inquisition, Crusades, Salem witch trials, both World Trade Center bombings, and countless others all fueled by hatred bred from religion. Up until the late 1700's people all over Europe were hung, be-headed, or burned at the stake for the belief that they were vampires, witches, and even werewolves.

After humans had stopped projecting the evil within them into other-worldly demons, we stepped backward in time and began demonizing our own kind. Vampires became people, humans that had died who were evil or base, supposed witches, or had died by suicide. This, of course, came from Christian teachings, but now the view was that vampires were once human beings who had turned to eating flesh and drinking blood after death because of a curse by Satan—since they lead a unholy or un-Christian life, they were doomed to be a earth-bound monster. The term vampire may be a recent addition to the myth, not even a thousand years old, but the mythos is ancient.

Other long-believed tales have a root in truth and is the smoke behind Bram's fire. It is one-hundred percent true that there was a man named Vlad Drakulya Tepes, Prince of Wallachia and ruler of Romania in the mid to late 1400's. His real name was Vlad Drakulya, which means "son of the dragon." The Tepes part he received after his death and means "impaler." He received this name for he defended his empire from the Turks and the Ottomans viciously and impaled the living and the dead upon long pikes and set them all about the countryside. He even piked his own people, all in an effort to dishearten and scare his enemies—a tactic that worked, for the invading Turks turned tail and retreated after seeing the gruesome handiwork of Vlad. It is said Vlad and his court had perfected the 'art' of impaling humans and it evolved because of his trial-and-error ways. You see…everything evolves.

Vlad is also known for murdering and piking not only his enemies, but many of his own people: ones that stole, lied, cheated, or disagreed with his policies or his humor. He would have victims boiled and/or roasted and then discreetly fed to their friends and family as "meat". Subjects were skinned alive, or had their feet skinned and then rubbed with salt, and others were drowned. What a nice guy, huh? He the thrice-deadly Hammurabi of his time, but it did keep Vlad's people in line and his enemies at bay. He was considered a demon of a man, and people had even said he was too evil to die; that even death would not stop his lust for blood. A few hundred years later, after staying a night in Vlad's abandoned castle, Bram Stoker made him even more famous.

The vampires that people believe in today are the romanticized versions, which are simply evolved characters from Bram Stoker's famous book, *Dracula*. The pale skin due to un-death, super-human strength and resilience, hypnosis, the loss of a soul and having no reflection, the affinity towards wolves and bats, the ability to shape-shift into both of these creatures as well as communicate and control them, an aversion to Christian holy symbols and water blessed by a priest, and to be able to fly and/or turn into mist are all thanks to Mr. Stoker. Let's look at vampires with our anti-theist goggles on and see what comes to light. Without gods and magic, the vampire becomes impossible. Either way, it is time to dissect what it means to be a vampire as we know it.

First of all, being a living dead is an oxymoron. If you are dead you cannot be alive and if you are alive your body is not dead. This cannot happen outside of magic and magic, as we now know, is not real. One of the traits of being a living dead is that you are 'alive' while your body is suspended somewhere between life and death—providing that your body has not decomposed at all. As such, an undead would have no metabolism. If a body has no metabolism, a whole slew of problems arise with being a vampire. No metabolism means that you do not breath, do not need sleep, do not get aches or pains and do not have bodily functions. If you do not breath there is no way for you to smell anything, make use of the diaphragm for speech, or supply oxygen to the rest of your body. If you have no metabolism than it makes sense your organs do not function and the only way to get around this is to have the ability to force your lungs and diaphragm to work with constant mental control. Without the aid of magic that is all impossible.

All of your body's major organs, including the brain, eyes, spinal cord and muscles need fresh blood and oxygen to function. "Well, that is why vampires drink blood, to supply their bodies with it." Alright, but a vampire can ingest all the flesh and fresh blood it wants, but with no metabolism how do you suppose that blood will be digested and distributed? "Well, vampires are called the living dead. They are dead but alive, so they must have some sort of metabolism." It makes little sense that a dead body has life in it, that a body is dead in terms of being alive yet dead for terms of metabolism and aging. This too requires special magic, for no natural phenomena can keep a body between life and death, especially selectively.

There are more downsides to having no metabolism: no metabolic function means no sex drive, no erections and no ejaculation. You would not feel any sensations, as your skin and nerves would not react to stimuli. Vampires always seem to heal very quickly, in some cases instantaneously. This suggests a highly-active metabolic system. It all requires very specific magic.

Onto the notion that vampires have no souls we encounter more problems. Who is the genius that came up with the belief that if a person's soul was to pass-on a body could not only still exist, but lose its ability to reflect itself in a mirror? Why in the world would a physical object lose any ability to have a reflection? I have formerly stated that I personally do not believe any living thing has a soul, but for argument's sake let me agree that I have a soul. If I were to die, would not my soul pass on? Would it not go where souls go, like Heaven, Hell, Purgatory, Valhalla, the Elysian Fields, or off into space? No matter how I did die my soul would go where souls supposedly go. If I were to die, my body would still have the ability to show up in a mirror and the ability to show up on film or on a video screen. If I was murdered and the authorities took photographs to study the case, they would be able to do so. In the case of a vampire, when the human being ceases being a human being and it transformed into a vampire, the soul supposedly leaves the body. Where it goes is not a factor, but what makes this any different than anyone else dying? A vampire, a soulless being, would still cast a shadow and have a reflection, or be able to be photographed. The only excuse or escape from this situation—allowing that vampires are real—is that the whole "not casting a shadow" thing was all wrong and just an incorrect myth about vampires.

Why would an undead being have super-human strength? If there is no metabolism there would be extreme rigor in the muscles. Even allowing for a vampire to have fluid movement, why would being dead greatly increase one's strength, bone, or muscle mass?

Shape-shifting into a bat, wolf, or mist form requires pure magic and something no non-magical being can do. I will get to shape-shifting after I have finished with vampires. The ability to hypnotize people and the ability to control bats and wolves can be either a magical effect or psionic (mind-generated) in nature and that too will be in a later chapter of this book.

Sunlight is the main enemy of the vampire; its rays cause it to burn and turn to dust, forever sending it to non-existence. My question is this: why does the light from the moon or the stars not do the same? Moonlight is simply reflected sunlight and the light from stars is the same type of light our sun can generate. Moonbeams should set a vampire afire as surely as sunlight would. Staking is the other bane of a vampire. Not much else (physically) can hurt them except beheading, but a wooden stake through the chest of heart does them in. This wives tale if from medieval Europe; dead people suspected to be vampires were thought to rise from their graves at night and drink the blood of the living. The superstitious nincompoops of the time figured if they dug up the corpse and saw evidence of life it meant vampirism and they could end it by staking the body down so it could not arise at night—it would be stuck. But did not a vampire possess super strength? How would a measly stake stop it? What these overly religious, non-educated people did not know is that a dead body can still grow hair, fingernails and toenails for some time. The buildup of gasses and the decay of tissue in a rotting body can create the illusion of distended body parts, like the stomach and intestines (not filled with the blood of the living, but gas of its own making), eyes, gums and teeth and lips. Any mouth that shows signs of decomposition will have receding gums. When gums recede, even the smallest of teeth will look bigger, and human canines will indeed look like elongated fangs when the gum line recedes. It was not signs of blood drinking these villagers saw, but signs of decomposition.

As for being harmed by holy items, it is the same old argument that I will re-use. Before the rise of Christianity vampires, in whatever form and names they were given, never suffered ill effects from having blessed water used upon them, or from holy symbols. It seems as if vampires are specifically tied to Christianity and to Satan, as they are un-holy, anti-Christian beings. Judaism and Islam, both share the tenant that no effigies or graven images of God shall be fashioned, and so both religions have no real holy symbol. I could get into a tirade about how Christianity breaks this (important) commandment over and over and over, but this book is not about religious inaccuracies and discrepancies. Do you ever wonder, however, why a vampire either would or would not cringe at a Star of David, or some sort of Islamic symbol pertaining to their lands and people. The Star of David is not a holy symbol, just the decoration of King David's empire. Though Israel and the Jewish people use it to represent themselves it is not in any way a symbol of Judaism.

If a vampire was attacking you, would you expect an American flag to cause it harm? Old Glory, the Red, White and Blue, represents America and its people, not a religion. The Star of David is the same. Since Christianity is the only one of these three intertwined religions to have holy symbols, it leads one to believe that vampires are a Christian problem and all of their problems start with Satan. The only *problem* is that vampires pre-date Christianity by too many thousands of years. As it adopted all of paganism that it encountered, Christianity adopted the vampire myths and legends inadvertently and its followers fashioned and formed them over time to conform to its teachings. Yet again, something else evolved.

Without gods and targeted, uniquely specific magic, vampires become moot. No natural evolution of man would allow for such wondrous (or accursed) gifts as the vampire is supposed to possess. Vampires are just not real. Humans who think they are vampires and want to act out and live out their fantasy or delusion is one thing, but Nosferatu and Dracula are nothing but tales of ancient fears, and story-book and silver screen myths.

*****

Werewolves were always my favorite. I recall, when I was a child, I would listen to the syndicated radio shows and play with my Legos.

Wolfman Jack was my favorite disc jockey and I really thought he was a werewolf. Why else would his name be Wolfman? I thought it was the coolest thing, to be a werewolf who had the rockin' job of playing music for millions of people instead of eating them. I wanted to be a wolfman DJ, too. Part of it is true today; I am a disc jockey in my spare time, but I do not terrorize people during a full moon and make them scream—I make them dance!

The myth of werewolves dates back to ancient times, to so far back in our history that no one really knows where it all started. Some claim it was in legends from ancient China were people were thought to be werefoxes and go out at night and have tea parties. Some claim it is from Greece, for the basis for many stories and myths sprout from Greek legends. The word werewolf is relatively new, a perhaps two-thousand years or so. It is, like the word vampire, a hybrid composite of mainly Germanic and English design. The words wair, werand verr are Germanic and Nordic and can all mean man. The word wulf means wolf. Varwulf, or wairwulf and verrwulf translate to werewolf in English.

Men have dreamed of and have been terrified of shape-shifting into animals since we were cave-dwellers. While the thought is actually pretty attractive, it is nothing but myth. Wolves have always scared man and long have the two shared a rocky path. We have competed with wolves for living space and for food up until the past one-hundred years or so. They have killed a number of us humans along the way and we have killed untold numbers of these magnificent predators. It is the way of humans, but this hatred and fear of wolves is what created the legend.

Not so much demons, as vampires were thought to be, people who could shape-shift into wolf form were altogether different. Some cultures saw shape-shifting as a boon, the power of a deft hunter and a powerful spirit. Other cultures made it into a terrible thing and that only evil, predatory people were afflicted with the curse of transforming into a beast. Others were simply innocent people believed to be cursed by being bitten by a wolf, or another werewolf, or had a magic spell cast upon them making them an unwilling shifter. In middle-ages Europe up through the

1700's, some people even believed they could make ointments and salves to transform themselves into werewolves.

A funny thing is that no one I have heard of seems to recognize that all known stories and accounts of werewolves through the ages (especially in books and movies) rest their laurels on men (very infrequently women) becoming a werewolf and terrorizing other humans. It is as if wolves care only for human flesh and the hunting and murdering of humans. Wolves have hunted humans throughout time and still do, but it is a rare occurrence. All wild canines would rather avoid humans as they have learned we are dangerous, as much as they are. It is in their genes and custom to avoid us, or so they have learned. Werewolves seek out only humans for prey. Why? It would make sense that if a human was turned into a wolf that its natural instinct would to go into the woods and hunt deer, or bison, or rodents. A werewolf would want to sniff out trees and bushes and rocks to mark them with urine or dung, not terrorize a village. You want to know why werewolves hunt humans? Humans are inherently chaotic, cruel, wild creatures, at least as far as I am concerned.

Human nature as we know it is one of selfishness and ego. Wolves hunt for food, not for sport. Wolves kill to eat, not to satiate urges for terror and dominance—that is what humans do, mostly the males. Just as the Christian deity is said to have made man in His image, human **men** have made werewolves in their image. The desire to be wild and strong, a cunning hunter and a devourer of the weak and lesser is what most men want. Human men love power, crave it like an addict craves heroin and get a natural high from it. Men, up until the early twentieth century, were at a stage when chivalry was all but dying, religion was still immensely able to destroy common sense and illiteracy was yet very prevalent. Up until the early 1900's the fearful ways of the old world could still play humans like a harp. Dating back to the first tale of werewolves, where men became animals and ate other humans, only tells us that cannibalism was a fearful yet evident truth of the world—better to become a monster and eat your fellow man then eat your fellow and be labeled a monster. It also tells us that deep inside males want to be animals; wild and free and immune to the law. A true werewolf would crave the hunt, but for food. If it took a human as prey it would be out of hunger, not malevolence.

The attributes of lycanthropes, or werewolves, as we know today have changed much over the centuries. Just like pop culture and Hollywood has done with the vampire, werewolves and the mythos about them has evolved over time. In tales of old, dating back to ancient times, werewolves were simple men or women (mostly men) who could transform themselves into wolves. By the time Rome arose to power, lycanthropy was seen as a curse—the Greeks and Romans did not assign any animal traits to their gods. Unlike almost every other world culture that had come before, the Greek gods possessed no animal-gods, no gods with animal traits and any such representation, was an offense to their sensibilities and culture. To a Greek or an ancient Roman, it was a curse to be transformed into a wolf, or to be able to commit the act. It was punishment by one of the gods. Moving forward in time to Christianized Europe, the same can be said. To Christians, being a werewolf was a curse from God, a punishment for evil thoughts, behavior, or for going against church dogma. Ha, ha—being turned into a canine for going against dogma. Kind of ironic, don't you think?

By the time of the middle-ages, werewolves were all thought of as evil, corpse-eating man killers. Even innocent people, some who did not know they were supposedly werewolves, would transform into a beast that wanted nothing more than to consume human flesh. These tales always bespoke of sad, melancholy people. "Normal", God-fearing people thought sad and depressed people were that way for they could not recall what they had done in wolf form. The geniuses of the time (those that lived in fear of the church and its clergy and were such easily incited people…so pretty much the entire population of the Christian world) would scour their villages for depressed, melancholy people and accuse them of being a werewolf. Like people thought to be witches and vampires, these people went though hellish trials that tortured and then killed them all in the name of God. Kill 'em all, let God sort 'em out is popular with most every religion it seems.

Werewolves of pre-modern day superstition possessed no real super-human attributes other than the ability to shape-shift. Up through the ages the powers of werewolves stayed at an even keel. It was for the late-era Europeans, just past the Victorian Era, that a werewolf's powers began to evolve. They became people capable of attaining a quasi-wolf yet still human form and their senses and physical nature were greatly enhanced. Their strength increased to super-human levels, their claws became strong talons capable of slicing as would a sharp blade.

Considering werewolves and other shape-shifters, one must consider again Einstein's law of conservation of mass/energy. Since energy cannot be created or destroyed and just changes form, where does the mass of a shape-shifter come from or go to? It must come from and go to somewhere. If a one hundred and eighty pound man transforms into a werewolf, the wolf must be equal to the same weight. If the same man becomes a wolf-humanoid hybrid, that is so popular in books and movies and is a larger being after his transformation, the mass has to come from somewhere. If all the extra bone, muscle, tissue, fur and blood that makes up the wolf-human hybrid exceeds the 180-pounds of our werewolf, that mass has to come from somewhere in the universe. It cannot come from nowhere and nothing. The opposite is someone transforming into a creature less massive than it begins. If a person is a werefox, a wererat, or can turn into a bat, the target loses mass when it shifts form. If our 180-pound man shape-shifts into a bat, he loses approximately one-hundred and seventy-five pounds or so. Where does that mass go? If it goes away somewhere, how does it return to the person when they again assume human form?

On this principle of physics it is not possible for a person to change into a creature that is more or less massive than it is to begin with. The only way, of course, is with magic and/or the aid of a deity. One of the only people to get the subject even closer to correct is Marvel Comics. As a comics fan I grew up on Spider-man, the Avengers and the X-men. The X-men had a constant pain in the butt named Mystique. Mystique is a mutant with the ability to shape-shift and can assume the form and characteristics (looks, skin tone, hair, voice, etc…) of anyone she meets.

Mystique is limited in her power for she can only move around her own mass and cannot add or remove it from her being. In other words, she has to work with what she has and cannot draw upon mass that is not there nor can she mysteriously shed it to an undisclosed area of space and time and recall it later.

In the case of a vampire who can supposedly turn itself into mist we face a new set of problems. Not only does a vampire need to magically add or shed mass, unless the mist weighs the same as the creature does, turning oneself to mist relinquishes all bodily functions, including brain activity. If one becomes a misty, inanimate being, it stands to reason that only force of will is holding the body together. What then of sentience? A cloud of vapor or mist has no brain and even a living dead would find it difficult to direct its movements with no spinal column, skeletal and/or musculature system. Painfully redundant is the fact that magic is required to accomplish such a transformation to and from mist form.

In nature, the moon plays such a vital role that without it life on our planet would be severely different—maybe even non-existent! From slowing down the speed at which the Earth spins to regulating oceanic tides, our moon works wonders. The moon has intrigued man for as long as man has been gazing at it. The same can be said of animals, but none more than the wolf. Wolves, foxes, coyotes and even your family dog are all canines, all descended from the same animal. All canines share an exact DNA profile and are the same aside from size, color and fur type. Why do canines howl at a full moon? What is it about a full moon that sets these animals off? That is one question that only dogs can answer, but is one that has spooked mankind since pre-historic times.

From monkeys to hominids and from hominids to modern man, wolves and humans (and our predecessors) have always competed for food and living space. Much more adapted for killing and surviving, wolves and humans have struggled with each other for millennia. They live on the outskirts of our societies, kill our livestock, occasionally have taken humans as prey and have always had an uncanny means of scaring the tar out of us. With their keen eyes that reflect light making them glow at night, their large teeth and feral ways and the way they seem to look into the (non-existent) soul of their prey, humans have always feared wolves. What is one of mankind's greatest abilities? To hate and demonize what we fear, and we did just that to wolves. What, then, was a more horrible fate for a human to suffer than to be a beast, a demon creature of the forest?

Like I stated before, native human tribes across the world (ones that did not suffer from Christianity) saw turning into a wolf, a jaguar, a bear, an eagle, as a grand convergence of human and nature, that Mother Earth or the gods deemed one worthy enough to be a great hunter. It is only the Mediterranean and European people (before and after Christianity) that made such an act a shameful, demonic enterprise. Greeks considered man above all animals and it was an affront to make men similar to beats just as it is an affront for certain religions to idolatrize. After Christianity spread it became not only an affront but a sin and the work of the Devil. For a person long to be a beast or to be cursed as a demon was the powers of Hell at work!

Silver…one of the only weapons humans had to use against a werewolf. Barring magic, the only explanation is that the act of shape-shifting alters a body's alchemical structure so that a severe allergy to silver is developed. That, of course, makes as much sense as a web-footed elephant. Silver was never a werewolf's bane until a few centuries ago when Victorian era Europeans stylized and evolved the werewolf mythos. Silver daggers, silver-tipped canes and silver bullets were what were said to do in a werewolf. If werewolves and other such creatures were considered demons, or cursed by Satan, why were holy symbols never used? They worked well enough against vampires, and werewolves go hand-in-hand with the living dead in respect to their nature as evil, devilish beings born of Hell. In any culture that thought werewolves in such terms is there any providence of holy water or the cross used as a deterrent. I find that odd.

Please allow me to deviate just a bit here and share my thoughts on the unnatural. Looking at vampires, werewolves, and any creature deemed unnatural from a Judeo-Christian standpoint just seems wrong. What I mean to say is that the logic is flawed. I will explain: God is the creator of all there is. That means God created all the good and all the bad—there cannot be any deviance from that. That means God created Satan in whatever form Satan first manifested in. If Satan was cast out from the kingdom of Heaven, He "fell" to Hell with whatever angelic powers God granted him. If Satan assumed additional powers when he fell, who granted these powers? Who else but God? If Satan just acquired them outside of God (very odd) it was still with God's full knowledge and these powers were never stripped.

Now, all that having been said, God created all there is, including magic/powers of darkness/curses or whatever you wish to call them. It also means God created demons, the undead, shape-shifters, monsters. If God created all of this, how can anything be un-natural? It was made by God, naturally. Even if Satan is responsible for magic, undead, werewolves, etc…it all came from God; Satan's powers were God-given, and so must be natural in nature. Henceforth anything Satan creates is created using the natural means available within the universe. The universe, the entire cosmos, and _every iota_ of creation were all naturally created by God.

What I am trying to get at is nothing can conceivable be un-natural: not magic and not _any_ creature …at least not if you believe in God. It boils down to choice of thoughts, and choice of action.

Back to our regularly-scheduled program: werewolves!

Very few of Hollywood's movies show a slow, painful transformation from human into a werewolf. I said a few, not any. _American Werewolf in London_ was one, and 2010's _The Wolfman_ is another, but most werewolf flicks show a fast, sometimes immediate shift from human to wolf. Even assuming magic and gods are real, a shift from human to animal has to be an agonizing experience; bone is folding, re-building and re-shaping. Muscles, tendons and ligaments are tearing way from bones to re-attach. Teeth and claws are sprouting—and humans have thirty-two teeth while dogs have forty-two. Ten more teeth have to grow from the jaw bones during a shift and ten more have to disappear when the werewolf shifts back. On top of that, teeth are enamel and not bone and enamel is only found in teeth, so where does the extra enamel come from?

At any speed it must be a painful thing to go through and all that body re-structuring has to take time. A fast shift just seems too fanciful.

Any shift is just too fanciful and the only conclusion to draw is that vampires, werewolves and other shape-shifters exist only in the movies and in minds, folk-lore and in stories crafted by excitable, blinded-by-faith, fearful, superstitious people.

Chapter Eight: Angels, Demons, & Chupacabra

Yes, it is quite odd to lump the Chupacabra in with angels and demons. What was that old Sesame Street gig? One of these things is not like the other…but I will get to why I have put the Chupacabra in this chapter a bit later, but first be aware that I almost included the subject of this chapter earlier, in chapter four. I later decided that it had enough merit to stand alone. First let me tackle the guys who stand on each shoulder when it comes time for a rough decision.

Angels and demons are not just a book by author Dan Brown. Long before Christianity mankind believed in angelic and demonic beings. This is a natural evolution of consciousness and of morals. There are always opposites: light and dark, right and wrong, Yin and Yang, good and evil*, Abbott and Costello…and angels and demons. Mankind has always found itself between a rock and a hard place after we formed rational, conscious thought. Humans tried to decide what was right and what was wrong by inventing religions, but they have yet to yield any results. Antitheists are the way they are not only to disavow archaic and ancient ideas, but to denounce morally bankrupt religions. The idea of angelic and demonic beings dates back as far as human history is concerned.

Humans are infamous for not wanting to be responsible for anything. It is just one of our unique and wonderful character traits. I believe it started as far back as when we came out from living in caves and formed our first societies. Our burgeoning brains were bursting with acquired knowledge of the world in which we lived, but our primal self-defense and preservation mechanisms were just too firmly ingrained in our beings. Selfishness (for survival purposes) and fear of the entire great, big unknown that was out there met a pass-the-buck attitude. From that sprang most all or our religions, but also our ability to project anything we found dismaying or bad that we did to an outside force.

It was easy for early man to assume that howling wind and the thunder and lightning were evil forces bent on destroying and causing havoc. It was understandable that wild animals with their fangs and claws and eyes that shone brightly at night—many with a taste for human flesh—could be made into horrible creatures. Our imagination, fueled by both fear and what we did not know, did the rest. By the time we humans could form complex thoughts we had created the first angels and demons, beings that were either in existence to perform good deeds and help us or beings that existed solely for maliciousness and to prey upon us.

Up through the eons and ages, as humans progressed and religions were born and died out, the idea of creatures of pure good or pure evil stayed with us and became stronger and stronger. Up above I placed an asterisk by the word *evil*. I did that because I want to explain my take on that word. I do not believe in the word evil and what it stands for as we understand it in relation to today's world. I say that because I also firmly believe that evil is not tangible and is not a force of the universe. I do not believe in evil men or evil creatures in as defined by religion. By nature I do not believe that living beings are evil. Evil is a mindset, a choice. We humans, in my humble opinion, have evolved past our basic human nature. We are now in a state of human behavior.

What the heck am I jabbering at? Certain things are human nature; hunger, sexual desire, self-preservation. Being evil is not in our nature. Religions would have you believe beyond a shadow of a doubt that the opposite is true. Even in Christianity, the supposed most enlightened, benign of religions, the basic tenant is that humans are born evil and horrible. What kind of foolishness is that? Evil is not in anyone's nature. Are lions evil because they kill every animal they can—including us—to feed themselves? Are wolves evil because they hunt to eat? Are hippos evil because they kill trespassing humans without a second thought and do not even eat them? Are whales evil because they kill fish to survive? Are humans evil, or are we basically good creatures?

Human beings are animals. We, like all other animals on this planet, are born apathetic creatures. Animals kill to survive—we need to eat and defend ourselves and when it comes to those two things it is done without a second thought by all species. What sets humans apart from the animal kingdom is that we have the ability to do "evil", while no animal does. Evil is not human nature, but human behavior. What I believe is that everything is a choice. It is not my nature to stab my neighbor in the eye with a pencil. It is not in my nature to murder someone for no other reason than my own wanting or for my religious beliefs. It is not in my nature to rape someone, or to go out and slash people tires, or to rob a bank. Those are all decisions I made on my own. They are not natural urges. A natural urge is to feel hungry when you see a commercial for a juicy hamburger. A natural urge is to get sexually exited when you see a very attractive member of the opposite sex (in my case, Jennifer Aniston or Beyonce certainly does the trick!) It is natural to slap a mosquito that is feeding off you and spreading disease. I keep saying that everything evolves and we humans have evolved beyond human nature and now have human behavior. I am also sad to say that our behavior, for the most part, is the pits.

But, yet again, enough of my own personal views.

By creating creatures such as angels and demons, humans could project all sorts of fears as well as responsibilities away from themselves. The Devil made me do it! is one such example. I did not rape and kill that young child, the Devil made me do it! I want no part in the responsibility of my crime. The flip side is that human self-esteem is also very low all the time, at least for the religious of the world. The same way they do not want to accept responsibility for the bad, they have a hard time believing they are capable of any good on their own. They give accolades to non-existent deities for great ideas, wonderful inventions, or skillfully done deeds. Likewise we invented creatures to help us in our daily trials: guardian angels.

It is humorous to hear people talk about guardian angels, how one helped save a life. People who believe in angels love to dole out accolades when something goes in their favor; "I survived that car crash," or "I won that lottery", or "this bad thing did not happen" all because of an angel watching over me. Yes, well I never, ever hear that same sort of person curse the supposed angel when something bad happens. I know if I believed in angels and something bad happened I would berate that angel until it pleaded for my forgiveness. Then again, these are the same people who instead blame a demon for the bad, but why not still blame the angel for not being powerful, smart, or crafty enough to outsmart or out do that demon? This is the mentality that comes from the severely shallow pool of knowledge that thanks a god for surviving when their home is torn apart by a storm or tornado yet does not acknowledge or get angered that the same supposed deity is the one who sent the storm in the first place.

Since gods and magic do not exist, neither do angels or demons. Or do they? One possibility is that angels and demons are extra-terrestrial beings, creatures that may have the technology to span the stars and reach other planets. Perhaps, way back in human history, we were visited by humanoids that possessed some of the physical traits we assign to angels and demons. Possibly the angelic visitors had wings, or wing-like apertures and were kind and benevolent visitors. Conceivably the demonic visitors had horns or spines, or prehensile tails, were malicious and did take humans by force for slaves, experiments, or for food. No one can support or deny such ideas for no one will ever really know, but these two scenarios are natural explanations for angels and now you understand why this chapter—minus all my views on morals, religion and human nature—could be in chapter four.

Another possibility, but not one I prescribe to, is that angelic and/or demonic beings come from another dimension. I, along with many scientists, do not buy the idea of multiple realities—not that I am a scientist or want to lump myself with these true geniuses—but that does not mean it is not possible from a natural standpoint. When our universe was created, by whatever means, is it beyond the scope of reason that multiple universes and multiple realities were also created? I do not have the definitive know-how to get into to this, but I treat it like all the rest of the oddities and mysteries out there; when I have proof that is not based on faith, belief, or "maybe" then I will concede. Until then I go on what we know to be true via science and physical proof, and right now both of those tell us that this universe is all we know and can study and so this universe is all I believe in. It is not that I am narrow-minded or too resistant to other ideas; on the contrary, as a fiction writer and a fantasy lover I would love for alternate realities and dimensions to be real. There seems to be only three ways to break the barriers between another universe/dimension and ours: natural phenomena, high technology and magic.

Right away I rule out magic, for I will never buy into the idea that words and gestures combined with burning wax and drawing arcane symbols, and possibly a blood sacrifice, can accomplish anything but waste time. Again, if such is true it means that the universe is one vast sentient thing that waits for living beings to utter the right words (causing the resonant harmonics required to trigger physics-defying effects), displace the air via gestures and burn plants and animals so that the universe can "smell" what is being burnt. The idea of any gods is ruled out as discussed before, especially God—it is the Judeo-Christian God itself that describes magic off limits. It stands to reason, from a theistic standpoint, that if God is real and did create all there is then He also created any and all other universes and dimensions. If that is true than all other forms of life are subject to the laws of God and magic would be off limits to them as well. That does not mean it cannot be used, it is just an offense to use it. But now we return to the earlier arguments of gods and God versus magic. Since all gods are not real and magic is not real, breaking the boundaries of realities using magic is not possible.

That leaves technology and natural phenomena as ways to travel between universes and dimensions. These are two highly-believable ways in which one could travel between realities, but they have yet to be proven. Saying technology can allow such travel is easy. Just as in science fiction books and movies, all we need to do is invent a machine to do it. Easier said than done.

Natural phenomena seem more plausible. The natural energies and happenings of the universe are more powerful and as-of-yet fully uncharted then we know. Take a star, for example. When a star "dies" it can become what we call a black hole. A black hole is when a star runs out of the fuel and energy it used to keep itself going. You must bear in mind that the matter of which stars are composed is very, very great. The material of a star's being is so dense that a simple teaspoon full would weigh as much as a mountain! When a star runs out of fuel, only its extraordinarily massive core is left, and it is so dense that it has a gravitational pull so strong that nothing escapes being in proximity to it— not even light. All matter and energy around the black hole is draw into its core, but where does it go? What happens to it? There are many theories and explanations and some suggest that traveling through a black hole may well deposit you/things in another reality/universe, or another part of space. As of yet it is all unknown. This is, however, an implementation of how one could travel to an alternate dimension or universe via natural phenomena.

Why all this scientific jargon? Well, my argument is that angelic and/or demonic beings could be explained (accepting a lack of both gods and magic) by a race of people who have either naturally, scientifically, or both, figured out how to open portals to our universe. This, of course, is only possible if there are multiple universes and dimensions…

And this is where the goat sucker comes in. Chupacabra is Spanish for *goat sucker*. There are reports from all over Pan and South America, as well is in the South West United States, of the Chupacabra. In South America the goat sucker is described as a smallish, demonic monkey/reptile-like creature that feeds on farm animals by drinking their blood like a vampire. It is said to come out at night and terrorize the countryside, kill livestock and leave grizzly remnants of its nocturnal activities. In the United States it is described as some sort of odd animal, like a mutated coyote, but it still has a penchant for blood. I have included the Chupacabra in this chapter for if there are multiple realities and universes it could be that the Chupacabra is from one of these and somehow became stuck here on Earth. I do not buy that, but it is possible.

Anything is possible, just highly unlikely.

It is also possible that the Chupacabra is an alien. Perhaps it is a bestial life form, like something an alien race would keep as a pet or minion. It is possible that, during a recent visitation by an alien race, this pet escaped and became stranded on our planet. Again, it sounds very improbable, but is it? It is more unlikely that the Chupacabra is a natural denizen of this world, for it runs into the same dilemma I find with Bigfoot and lake monsters; it needs to have more of its kind to breed and has to hunt and it has to die. There would be wide-spread evidence of this creature unless it possesses intelligence far greater than we humans do and can easily elude, out-think and out-maneuver us at every turn. Very doubtful!

There are also many reports of the Chupacabra in Puerto Rico and conspiracy theorists claim the beast comes from the military base found there, isolated on a jungle mountain. Their theory claims that the creature is either an aberration, an experiment gone wrong with the beast escaping, or an alien that was held within the base that had escaped. I doubt both of those and the easiest explanation is that the Chupacabra is just not real, that it is an elaborate hoax that has easily fooled simple farmer folk and one that has grown way out of proportion. My own thoughts are that where there is smoke there is fire, but in this case the fire has roots in the natural world. Perhaps a local monkey, like a gibbon or howler monkey, was born deformed or became diseased. Superstitious and always fearful people can easily conjure demons out of the mundane and if they saw a deformed or diseased large monkey their fears exaggerations would grow and grow with each recounting of the tale.

Out of all the crazy South American Chupacabra stories the only one that even makes some semblance of sense is an experiment gone wrong. I fully believe it is possible that a government could have been conducting genetic tests on apes and monkeys in areas of the world where such goings on are easy to hide. If one of these aberration experiments did manage to escape into the countryside...Chupacabra! I like my own theory better, but one never knows.

As for the American, dog-like Chupacabra...you have to be kidding me. Name one canine in the natural world that eats its prey by tearing out a victim's throat and lapping up only blood. Name one. Can't do it? That's because the only mammal to do this is a vampire bat—not the tearing out of the throat, but the survival akin to Dracula. Canines eat everything, as we all know. They survive on flesh and bone, not blood. They are also smart creatures, but not smart enough to evade our detection for all these years, at least not living in the Southern deserts and scrub lands of the United States.

The American Chupacabra is very real. It is most likely a new breed of wild dog, one that has been breeding with coyotes and has contracted a deformity that is now part of its hereditary genetic code. It is probably a low population of creatures that may be overly prone to mange and other diseases along with its deformity. It is the smoke behind the fire, at least in my opinion.

Chapter Nine: Atlantis & the Bermuda Triangle

There is so much controversy about both of these subjects, so many books out there by noted and un-noted authors that I do not want to and in many cases cannot, match wits with. I base my simple solutions off what we know is true and what is untrue and what we know is physically and scientifically possible. On top of that I wear my godless, magic-less glasses to help me see things in a different light.

Atlantis is said to be an ancient Greek island nation that has since disappeared beneath the waves of the mighty ocean. Its people were said to be hundreds, perhaps thousands, of generations ahead of the people living at the time in respect to society and technology. We should even believe that they had a form of technology to rival what we now possess. For whatever reason or offense the city was wiped clean and was sunk into the sea. Gone are the splendors of Atlantis. Gone are the medical and technological breakthroughs these people are said to have acquired.

I look at Atlantis this way: Greece and the Greek islands lay in a vicinity of the world that has seen some amazing changes in the past few million years, and much of it moderately recent in terms of geologic time. The area has been created, submerged, risen from the sea like a phoenix from its own ashes and been subject of massive volcanic eruptions. It is wholly and undoubtedly possible that Atlantis, or a city nation of some sort, existed and was wiped away by Mother Nature. Volcanoes and under-sea earthquakes do have a tendency to destroy real estate indiscriminately, efficiently and rather quickly. In the Mediterranean volcanoes have done some major damage over the centuries. Two noted disasters in the region are the eruptions of Santorini and of Vesuvius. Santorini is the elder, having erupted some 3,700 years ago and is also called the Minoan Eruption. It erupted with such force and power that it blew chunks of earth, rock, magma and ash as far away as the Nile Delta—all the way in Egypt (which is in North Africa). The more famous eruption of Mount Vesuvius destroyed the island city of Pompeii, Greece, in 79 A.D. The city was buried under sixty feet of volcanic ash and debris and was not re-discovered until the late 1700's. I have been there; it is still beautiful and I can only imagine what it was like when it was a thriving place.

The point here is that the Mediterranean is a hotbed of volcanic activity. Maybe not as much as the South Pacific, but enough to note that many islands and cities have been claimed by Mother Nature. It is within reason to believe that an island nation like Atlantis could have existed and been destroyed by a volcanic eruption, which usually leads to a tsunami. What is not in the realm of credibility is that its inhabitants were some special people capable of producing technology that, even by today's standards, is pure science fiction.

Atlanteans were said to either be human-like aliens, or descendants of the Greek Titans and had harvested the power of pure energy, able to focus such energy through crystals and gems to power all sorts of amazing machines. They could levitate and fly with them as if they possessed some anti-gravitational ability. The crystals could be used as laser beams to cut and shape stone, or perform delicate surgery. Atlanteans could control the weather and other forces of nature, like volcanoes and the oceans themselves. Ironic that it is the same forces that supposedly destroyed the city.

Even saying that the Atlantean people were not aliens or demi-gods lends no credence to the theory of their technology. I do not mean to be cruel or overly-critical, but I never bought into the supposed "wisdom of the ancients." Pre-modern era humans were not smarter or less intelligent than we are now; they just knew less about their world. Humans have had the same brains and same brain capacity since were Cro-Magnon man; we just know more each year about our world and the physics that govern the universe. To say that the ancients had a wisdom that is lost to the world is almost an insult to modern science. By Zeus himself—we did not even put two and two together and place hygiene, or lack thereof, with plague, disease and sickness until a hundred or so years ago.

Ancient man was crafty with what was available at the time. They were capable of great feats, like moving monoliths and huge stones and crafting amazingly accurate structures as with the pyramids, but that does not make them wise. These same people who were so "wise" either thought the world was flat, that killing hundreds of people a day would appease the sun, that giant men with one eye stalked the land and buying, selling and keeping slaves was good living. Even today as smart as we are we are the dumbest creatures around. Humans are the only creatures to willingly take life-threatening risks for amusement. We are the only creatures that knowingly poison our bodies with alcohol and drugs and then have the audacity to call them diseases and also be appalled when we or someone we love gets sick and dies as a result. We are the only race to constantly hate, and to war and kill for simple beliefs. Mankind has never been wise save for a few handful individuals out of tens of billions over the course of human history. The ancients were not wise, just cunning and ingenious with the tools and resources at their disposal.

There are many people and noted scientists who point to all sorts of under-sea discoveries, like crystal-topped pyramids, ruined cities and roads all swallowed the ocean for evidence of Atlantis. Like I said, islands come and go and it means nothing to our planet. The earth itself is as apathetic to life as the entire universe is. The most reasonable explanation is that Atlantis was a real place, a real island with real humans upon it. These humans, as smart as their Greek counterparts, no more and no less, were wiped away by both an under-sea earthquake and its following tsunami or by a volcanic eruption. The other side of that coin is that the entire Atlantis myth is just a myth, hobbled together from bits and pieces of history so old that is pre-dates the written documentation and then is romanticized or embellished by more modern scribes and sages.

*****

The Bermuda Triangle is barely worth the effort to get into. I am sad and sorry for all the loss of life due to this natural phenomenon, but it does not mean there is much to say about it. What we call the Triangle, also the Devil's Triangle, is an area of ocean in the North Atlantic. It starts at the southern tip of Florida, extends to the island of Bermuda, down to Puerto Rico and back to Florida to form the triangle. Over the years numerous air and sea vessels have disappeared here. Some went down into the depths quickly and mysteriously, some are said to have just disappeared into the clouds. People believe that time can stand still here and that—possibly—the air and sea crafts that vanish in the Triangle get lost in time, or as Kurt Vonnegut would say, "unstuck in time."

To assume that an area of our world is maliciously intent on sinking ships, taking aircraft from the sky and killing people is ignorant. That scenario assumes that not only the universe is conspiring against us, but our own planet is as well…but only in this one tiny area over the ocean. To assume an alien spacecraft or object is sunken in the depths and is responsible for all the mayhem is ridiculous (see chapter four). To assume a man-made object is sunken in the depths and is responsible is also ridiculous. To assume that our world is capable of odd, strange natural phenomena is right on target. Magnetic forces, gravitational forces and solar radiation all play havoc on our little blue orb and some areas of it are more receptive to phenomena and disruption of the norm. The Bermuda Triangle is just one of them. These natural forces do not play well with others at times, and those "others" are our sophisticated yet delicate navigational instruments and craft they control.

Chapter Ten: Mental Powers

Scientists say that humans only use ten percent of our brains. We have a great potential and an untapped well of power just waiting to be accessed. Ruling out magic, the power of the human mind is said to a great and wondrous thing. As a comic book fan, I enjoy nothing more than a good story, especially one of vast mental prowess. I do not believe in it, but I enjoy it. Let me correct myself; I do not believe in it as far as humans are concerned. It is true that some animals have mental powers that we humans will never have. Bats, dolphins and whales all possess internal sonar, the ability to produce sound waves to scan and mentally shape surrounding areas by using their vocal chords, ears and brains. These animals can even use this sonar to stun prey items and then predate them. It is an amazing ability. It is undoubtedly possible that if complex life on another planet exists then at least one species possesses internal sonar like the animals listed above do. This life form could be an animal or a sentient being. As far as I am aware and concerned, humans do not possess nor will they ever possesses internal sonar.

Does that mean we humans do not possess other mental powers? Of course not…at least not yet; we are an evolving species. If we do possess any sort of mind power it must be in the budding stage and is most likely barely controllable on our end. There are many types of proposed mental powers: telekinesis is the ability to move objects with the mind. Pyrokenesis is the power to start fires with the mind. Telepathy is the ability to send, receive and or read thoughts with only the mind. Precognition is the ability to see the future while post-cognition is the ability to see events exactly as they unfolded in the past, as if the pre-cog was attending the event. Astral projection is the supposed ability to enter a trance-like state and have your consciousness leave the body and be able to travel about. Some claim to be able to breach the barrier of realms via astral projection. Channeling is the supposed ability to commune with spirits, ghosts and the dead. Since we have already discussed ghosts and spectral beings this one is not deserving of any attention…or is it?

There are more, but these are the most popular. Of these powers, the only one I can remotely believe that we are capable of is channeling, but in my own, twisted way of conceiving it. I have already explained why [sentient] ghosts are an impossibility, but I did agree that humans are made up of energy. If human [psychic] energy can "stain" our reality, could another human pick up on that energy and somehow commune with it? Perhaps commune is a bad choice of words. I would say read, tap into, or have empathy with rather than commune. It is entirely possible to perceive energy using only our minds, but energy does not have an agenda, emotions, or purpose. Energy just is, but perhaps someone who can channel can read this human energy stain and empathize with it and feel some of what its former human self was feeling, like sorrow, joy, anger, or any of the basic human emotions. I do not believe that a channeler could read an energy stain and discern pertinent, detailed, or graphic information, or that the energy stain could be remotely possible of any conscious thought or agenda. The stain, if real, is more of an inanimate object containing some information not unlike a data disc a computer could read.

When it comes to the other above mentioned mental powers, they are just too spectacular to be real, at least by human standards. Again, growing up reading comic books I know all about the various mental powers said to exist. Numerous books devoted to telekinetic, pyrokenetic and telepathic powers have been written by highly intelligent people, but in the end there is just no proof. After all the studies, all the tests, with all of our technology and all of our probing there is as much proof of mental powers as there is of gods, leprechauns, and unicorns. That is all that really matters at this point in time. Show me the money, right? The proof is in the pudding and faith in mental powers is not possession of mental powers. If we humans are still alive in a million or so years, we can re-visit this chapter and see if I am/was wrong.

If any beings on this planet would develop mental powers I would think it would be found in the animal kingdom and not the human one. As

I had said, bats and dolphins and whales possess natural mental powers. Sharks and other fish can uses senses to see and feel the magnetic lines and fields that abound on our world. Humans are the ADD subjects of planet earth and do not have nearly the mental stamina of most all animals. Watch a lion as it stalks prey or a shark as it tracks a seal. View a praying mantis as it lays in wait for a victim. Take note of how animals deal with pain, inclement weather and life-or-death situations, and you will find that their minds, although less evolved than our own, are more adept at almost anything. We humans may be smarter, but we are not as tough mentally nor as determined as our animal cousins.

When a lion stalks prey, it does not stare off at a butterfly as it flits from flower-to-flower. It does not get bored and begin to watch hyenas at play. No, it stares intently at its prey, as if mentally wishing the animal to just keel over or to be vexed, like Count Dracula would charm a hapless maiden. If any animal would develop telekinesis and or telepathy it would be the various predatory animals of the world. *I want that meal! Come to me! Break a limb so you cannot escape ~ snap! A bone cracks. Trip! Do not run! Die!* Then again, a prey animal could also develop these powers to ward off attack. *I am not the droid you are looking for (in its best jedi impression). Hunt another animal. You do not see me here in the tall grasses. There, take that old buck and not me. Shoooom! ~ I mentally push you away from me.*

Animals always follow through, because it means life or death. They may not succeed in their diligence, but they try like hell and with more mental effort than us more evolved and bigger-brained humans normally put in.

Chapter Eleven: Karma, Luck, and Superstations

What goes around comes around, or so it is supposed to be in this universe. Do I, as an anti-theist believe in that? Nope—at least not in the religious or sentient way. I do not believe that any god or gods are looking at our deeds and rewarding or punishing us for them, especially the little things. I do not believe that the universe is sentient and acts in the same fashion and notes when we hold a door for an old lady or purposely kill a lady bug. I do believe that what you give is what you get and what you do comes back to you in a comical sense of cosmic justice. It is more live by the sword, die by the sword in my eyes. You can go your whole life holding doors for old ladies, being careful not to kill a lady bug, being polite and kind and sensitive and smiling and still be killed by a bus or a rogue water buffalo, just as you can go through life being an insensitive prick who is filled with hatred, who never holds doors and kills animals for fun and lives a long, healthy life. The universe just does not give a rat's behind about us. If you live a decent life, smile and be nice it will rub off here and there. Not everyone is a prince or princess and not everyone is a saint, but the more people that are nice makes this world a better place.

It is not unlike this scenario: you own a small company that needs a hundred employs to operate. Let's say your company makes widgets. You need to manufacture and then sell the widgets to make a profit. If you hire too many people that are inept at the job of making widgets, you have surrounded yourself with less than sufficient help. If you do not release these people from your employ and hire people qualified to make your widgets, it is your fault. If you hire and surround yourself with good help, they will produce good products for you and your company will operate in the black. If you hire unqualified and poorly motivated people who cannot tell a widget from their elbow and then do nothing about it, you are to blame. The same holds true for real life; if you surround yourself and associate with decent people you will more than likely have a good and decent life. If you associate with bad, rude, bitter, criminal people you will live such a lifestyle.

You can, of course, do all the right things and still have life bite you in the rear. That is the random, chaotic universe being its apathetic self. You could be a saint of a person and still be murdered by a sociopath, raped by a low-life, or have your spouse killed by a careless drunk driver. The opposite is that you could be a murdering, raping drunk that sees ninety-five healthy years of life. If karma were truly real the universe would be a much different place. If gods are indeed real, well, as Ricky Ricardo would say, "they have some 'splainin to do."

Luck of the draw. The luck of the Irish. Beginner's luck. A lucky horseshoe. Lucky number seven. There are many more ways in which a person can be lucky. Breaking a mirror. Crossing the path of a black cat. Walking under a ladder. Opening an umbrella indoors. Stepping on a crack. There are many more ways people can be unlucky. I do not believe in luck much the same way I do not believe in karma. I do not think the universe is out to get us just as it is not looking out for us. Without gods one would be forced to believe that the universe is sentient and gives a hoot what befalls everything in it. Luck is just another word for chaos. A coin can land only one of three ways when tossed in the air; heads, tails, or somehow manages to land ridge-side up. It is not luck which way the coin lands, but chaos. Luck actually falls into two categories: luck itself and also superstition. The belief in luck, or believing items or events can change the path of things to come, is so ingrained into human culture that it is a religion unto itself. The problem with luck, however, is that people rarely stop and question the logic of luck, just as they rarely question the logic of religion.

One question to ask is who has the authority to decide what is lucky and what is not? A rabbit's foot is lucky, but for whom? Certainly not the rabbit. A horseshoe facing a certain way is lucky and unlucky when faced in another, but why? Who decided that to walk under a ladder is bad luck? That one is probably the easiest the understand; after the invention of ladders people must have always walked under them unbothered, but over time it is evident that the items people held while upon these ladders would fall, or be let go of and—*boink*–people get knocked on the noggin. It then was deemed that to walk under a ladder is unlucky whereas it should have been deemed just plain dumb.

For a long time Europeans deemed cats as evil, demonic, disease-spreading creatures. This of course was only after Christendom had come to Europe. Black cats especially were demonized and all manner of house cats were tortured and killed through Europe's long and blood-stained history. These God-fearing, Satan-fearing, everything-fearing people thought they were doing their deity's work by destroying cats by the thousands and that this would bring about good luck. What these simpletons blinded by their faith did not know is that the Black Death— the bubonic plague of the Dark Ages—was spread by infestations of vermin in the cities. The unchecked number of rodents carried with them billions upon billions of mites and fleas that helped spread the plague and kill off nearly four hundred million people.

Gee…what animal routinely hunts and eats vermin? What animal, aside from snakes, made its home in the cities of Europe and could have helped lessen the spread of the plague and save untold millions, perhaps? What animal did the fearful Europeans kill by the thousands? Yes, cats. It turns out that destroying so many cats was bad luck and a foolish move to boot. If karma is real then the Europeans got what they deserved, whether they knew better or not. If gods are real then they were apathetic to both the plague and its innocent victims and the slaughter of so many innocent animals. The ancient Egyptians revered cats as protectors of man and of holy places. Too bad the God-fearing people of Dark Ages Europe did not feel the same way.

Who decided that to break a mirror is bad luck and that it warrants seven whole years of trouble, or that to open an umbrella indoors was unlucky? What happened before the invention of mirrors and umbrellas and then their consequent invention? Did the person who invented the umbrella know it would be an item that would be unlucky to open inside a building? Why is a clover that has four leaves lucky but an animal that has two heads or an extra limb an aberration?

As for people, who coined the "luck of the Irish"? Is that to mean that Irish people are naturally lucky while all non-Irish people are not? We all get sick. We all get cancer, are born blind or deaf, get hit by buses, die in plane crashes, get divorced and lose at poker. The Irish do not have a monopoly on luck; they suffer the effects of universal chaos just like all of us humans do. The Jewish people are said to be the "chosen" people. By that I would take it to mean not only lucky, but to have a god on your side at all times. Aside from the above Irish reference, so many unlucky events have befallen the Jewish people that I would seriously doubt their status as "chosen", unless they were "chosen" to be sufferers and unlucky…and if a god is involved, what does that say? Nothing good in my humble opinion.

Certain numbers are lucky while others are deemed unlucky. Seven is seen as a lucky number, so would not multiples of seven be that much luckier? Seven is lucky, so shouldn't fourteen be extra lucky? What then of twenty-eight, fifty-two and so on? It would be infinite. Thirteen is unlucky, as is Friday the 13th and do you know why? No one really does, but before the nineteenth century there are no mentions of this day being unlucky. The Norse feared that thirteen people eating at a dinner table spoke of death the next day and Jesus was said to be executed on a Friday. It is also to be noted that Jesus had twelve disciples and when Judas showed up as an unofficial 13th dinner guest…well, you do the math. Carrying on, the number twenty-six should be doubly unlucky and so on. An interesting side note is that a deck of cards is said to possess a lot of luck. There are four suits of cards, each suit having thirteen cards. A complete deck with no jokers is fifty-two cards, a multiple of thirteen. How can it possibly be lucky unless it is all bad luck?

The bottom line is that luck is not real in any sense other than metaphorically. Superstitions should have no place in the logical and rational mind. Ladybugs are cute and beneficial to gardens, but killing one will not bring a black cloud over your head. Knocking on wood* will not appease the universe and bad things will not happen if you say something without knocking on wood. If something happens to go your way and you like its outcome and effect, it is good luck just as the opposite is bad luck. Wearing a dead animal's painted foot, or hanging a U-shaped piece of iron right-side up and not stepping on a crack in the pavement will do nothing to change the outcome of things. Opening an umbrella while inside a house, or breaking a piece of heated and painted sand (a mirror), or having an apex predator (a cat) cross your path will not anger the universe so that it plots against you. There is no agenda behind chaos, no cosmic conspiracy and no hidden meaning the way things turn out. They either benefit us or they do not. People just need to realize that, as Forrest Gump so eloquently said, shit happens.

*****

"If something is meant to be..." I hate that expression, but because of all unsaid bad that goes with the statement that no one talks about. Fate is something in which I do not prescribe to. Nothing is meant to be. If it is, than all the gods be damned! All of them. Suffering is meant to be? Disease and birth defects are meant to be? Broken hearts, broken bones, and broken homes are all part of the divine plan? A child dying young or a criminal dying old; a tunnel collapsing on a motorist's car where the car is cleaved in two and the man survives but his wife is made into paste (happened a few years ago in Boston); a father building a tree house for his kids that gives way and kills the children; a baby killed when it climbs onto a windowsill and falls to its death. The list goes on for infinity. If that is all meant to be, what does it say of the god(s) who decide such actions and outcomes? It says nothing good at all.

Nothing is meant to be except for the random, apathetic chaos of the universe. Nothing happens until one makes it happen. Do not pray for a cure for cancer, work for one. Do not hope for that person you like at work to ask you out, ask them out! Do not wait for your child to fall out of the window, secure it so that cannot happen. Do not worry about shoddy tunnel construction for you have no control over poorly made rivets and rust. Fate is not real, and another line from a movie (Terminator II) fits wonderfully: "No fate but what we make."

*Knocking on wood comes from the ancient English countrymen; the pagan druids, the same people who built Stonehenge. The pagans revered the world and everything had a spirit. Fey creatures, like nymphs and pixies, were said to dwell inside of trees, especially ash, oak, apple and birch. If a person happened by a tree and used it for, say, shelter from the rain or the sun, or for food, or for safety, or even just to take a nap, it was considered polite to knock on the tree a few times to let the nature spirit know you were there. The knock signified you giving thanks for the tree's presence, to the spirit.

Chapter Twelve: The End of the World (and this book)

Every culture has an end of times scenario. Human beings, preoccupied and scared witless of death have instilled and end of times story into nearly every religion they have made. The fierce Norse Vikings had Ragnarök, when the giant serpent that coils about the earth, Jörmungandr, would writhe and thrash and destroy the globe while the gods warred and mostly all died. The Jews believe that the world will last for but six thousand years and then a great war will come and God will save only the Jews. Buddhists believe that after five thousand years (or a longer period of time) people will stop practicing Buddhism and the world will fall into moral and sexual depravity. The combined sects of Christendom believe that Jesus will come back to earth and He will wage a war, and then the Rapture will happen; only the true believers and the "saved" will be spared and will enter heaven. The Maya believed that the universe will go through many changes and in December of 2012 A.D. the universe (as we know it) will either end or change so drastically that life will end. Hindu's have an end times, American Indians have one, Rastafarians have theirs, Islam has one and so on. Everyone has their spoon in the pot.

Christians, Mormons and Jehovah's Witnesses seem to be the ones who relish this event the most. They look forward to it and seem to not be able to wait for Jesus to return and smite and kill and maim and destroy. They constantly parade and picket and attest that the world will end and seem disappointed when events like Y2K pass without the return of the Messiah and blood does not run in the streets.

Humankind's biggest fear is death and our biggest enemy is ourselves. Oh, the world will end; that is true. It will not be when a mythical carpenter returns with a blood-seeking blade, or when a world-spanning snake decides to crush us in its grip, or when people stop practicing the ways of an ancient and kind monk, or one of the various deities created by man gets irked enough to wage a war. It will not end because people partake in sexual acts, or use narcotic substances, or gamble. It will not end when we (one day, but hopefully not) bomb ourselves into oblivion with nuclear weapons—human life may end because of that, but the earth and sky will endure and life will go on. The world will end in roughly five or six billion years from now, when our own sun dies and goes nova. It will turn the planet into a hostile, sterile husk for a few hundred thousand years or so and then it will finally melt and be crushed, along with our closet planetary kin, into space dust when the heat and gravity of our dying sun become so incredibly immense...and then nothing will be wasted, for the universe recycles everything. New worlds and new life will one day, no matter how inconceivably long it takes, form from our demise. Ashes to ashes and dust to dust, we will die but the universe will go on because it must.

In Closing

I hope the universe is a little bit less mysterious for you, at least in a good sense. It is mystery and the unknown that drives human science and build human knowledge. We know so much yet we know next to nothing. What we do know must be used for the common good. It must be used in combination with the smarts we possess and not trod upon ancient superstitions or by outdated and any and all morally bankrupt religions. There are indeed mysteries that abound on this blue-green globe we live upon, but when you think of the ones we dwell upon with rationality and critical thought, you come up with the answers I have assigned to them, as you have just read. There are great mysteries to be deciphered, decoded and explored, but ghosts, lake monsters, ape-men, man-made deities and other subjects that I touched upon should not be on that list; fine, they can be, but not much time or effort should be expended upon them. There are greater mysteries, like why is it that I put two socks into my washer and dryer yet only one comes out? Who is Captain Crunch, in whose navy did he serve and why was he relegated to a ship full of cereal? When will humans stop hating and killing each other over the color of skin, for pieces of green paper or for shiny rocks, or simply believing something different than what the other believes? Those are the serious questions that need answering and are some of the true mysteries of the universe as I see it.

About the Author

J.M. Ladd lives with his wife, son, and flying Yorkshire terrier. He likes to read, write, play poker, and to research mythology, dinosaurs, and human history. He hopes you have enjoyed this book and that it made you think, laugh, or both.